Appetite for Murder

A Mystery Lover's Cookbook

Kathy Borich

"Appetite for Murder," by Kathy Borich. ISBN 1-58939-499-2.

Published 2003 by Virtualbookworm.com Publishing Inc., P.O. Box 9949, College Station, TX, 77842, US.
©2003 Kathy Borich. All rights reserved. No part of this publication may be reproduced, stored in a retrieval system, or transmitted in any form or by any means, electronic, mechanical, recording or otherwise, without the prior written permission of Kathy Borich.

Manufactured in the United States of America.

This book is dedicated to my mother,
who instilled in me a love
for the art of cooking
and the beauty of literature.

At a Glance

Contents

Sir Arthur Conan Doyle

A Hearty Hunter's Supper with Holmes and Watson

Like many of the big events in history, "The Adventure of the Noble Bachelor" begins with a wedding. We're not talking the golden apple and Trojan War here, but a "singular occurrence at a fashionable wedding," namely, the sudden disappearance of the bride.

Our menu includes *Grilled Quail Salad with Tarragon Citrus Vinaigrette, Brandied Pate de Foie Gras Pie, Smothered Pheasant in Sherry Cream Sauce, Pan Seared Venison with Wild Mushrooms and Chili Glaze,* and *Wild Rice and Pecan Pilaf.*

Strange Birds and Bedfellows

In "The Adventure of the Blue Carbuncle" we find our purloined gem tucked away in a very seasonal pocket – the crop of " a most unimpeachable Christmas goose."

Our menu includes *Roast Christmas Goose with Apricot-Port Glaze, Cracked Wheat and Apricot Stuffing, New Potatoes in a Lemon Chive Sauce, Cold Asparagus in Walnut Drizzle,* and *Watercress Fennel Salad with Tarragon-Rosemary Vinaigrette.*

Indian Spice and Everything Nice

Huddled in the first class carriage – we can almost hear the clacking of the rails and feel the steady vibration of the train – Holmes leans forward with his sharp and eager face to explain the facts of the case to Watson – the disappearance of the Wessex Cup favorite, Silver Blaze, and the mysterious death of its trainer, John Straker.

Our menu bubbles over with seventeen exotic spices. In addition to the *Kasmiri Griddle Kabobs,* it features *Vegetable Pulao, Broccoli with Peanuts, Ginger, and Indian Spices; Prawn Balchow,* and *Grape Raita with Cilantro, Mint, and Green Chile Spiked with Yogurt.*

Dinner at the Diogenes Club with Mycroft Holmes

A giggling villain with cold, steel-grey eyes. A damsel in distress held captive in a dark, deserted house, her brother slowly starving to death for his refusal to sign away the family fortune. What a stew of melodramatic moments!

We will feast upon *Golden Rissoles with a Port Cumberland Sauce, Mushrooms in Sherry Cream, Carrottes a la Flamande,* and *Blanc Mange in Custard Sauce.*

> *It's always better when it happens on a train. Whispered words of passion muffled by clacking wheels, narrow lovemaking in the upper berth, a grisly murder behind polished mahogany.*

Feast your eyes upon the polished silver trays, the crisp white linens, the gleaming crystal, and join Hercule Poirot for an exquisite meal of *Sole Marguery in Wine Sauce, Spinach Crepes, Pommes de Terre Lyonnaise,* and *Apple Cream Steeped in a Lemon. Thyme, and Rosemary Wine Sauce.*

Margery Allingham

> *That unscrupulous art dealer has cooked up one fantastic scam. Now this clever killer has invited you into his lair. The game is up and you both know it. But don't be put off by little things, like death staring you in the face.*

Enjoy the elegant dinner at fabulous Savarini's as though it's your last as you nibble on *Mushroom Omelettes in Port Sauce, Tournedos Macconnaise,* and *Veal Sweetbreads in the Basque Style.*

Dorothy L. Sayers

> *Is it the kiss or the ham sandwich? Let's start with the kiss. Now he may look a little ridiculous to us today. I mean what hunk wears a monocle! But in his own way Lord Peter is loaded with sex appeal.*

Let's get our picnic off to a great start with some tips on picking the Quintessential Ham as well as an ode to the gastronomical delights of real *Dijon Mustard.* Complete your epicurean meal with *Golden Cheese Soufflé with Peppery Bacon,* and *French Potato Salad Bathed in Vermouth, Chervil, Chives and Tarragon.*

John Mortimer

> *Horace Rumpole is not particularly thrilled with "wafer thin slices of anything," and he thinks crime is a more honest type of robbery than the prices at La Maison Jean Pierre. Its haughty chef must eat some humble pie before Rumpole agrees to take on his case.*

Rumpole's dinner features *Steak and Kidney Pud with Mashed Spuds on the Side.* We'll round that out with more of Rumpole's favorites, like *Shepherd's Pie,* and close with that curiously named fruity pudding, *Spotted Dick.*

Colin Dexter

> *Slowly he becomes obsessed with a long forgotten crime. From his hospital bed Morse sets out to prove the innocence of two men hanged in 1859, exercising only, as Poirot called them, "the little grey cells."*

Our meal features that decadent fried English classic, *Fish and Chips,* served up with plenty of grease and washed down with as many pints of ale as necessary. We've even thrown in a few other pub delicacies with those strange names, like *Toad in the Hole, Bubble and Squeak,* and *Bangers and Mash.*

> *Quite a grisly scene, their last supper. Three plates of food, cold and congealing, like the blood that sauces them. Chief Inspector Reginald Wexford will have to wade through two more corpses, one hanged and one burnt, before he finds the killer.*

Our Sunday dinner features *Roast Beef with Yorkshire Pudding and Browned Roast Potatoes*, as thoroughly British and old fashioned as Wexford himself. Let's begin with *Hearty White Wine and Garlic Soup*, then on to *Fresh Mushroom Salad with Watercress and Scallions*. With our main course try a nice portion of *Leeks au Gratin*, and close with a dessert of exquisite lightness itself, *Melon with Strawberries and Anisette*.

> *From the musty darkness of his haunted mansion, Inspector Dupin unravels a case of graphic violence. A mother and daughter are brutally hacked to death, bloody clumps of human hair yanked out by the roots, and one of the corpses stuffed up the chimney.*

We've prepared the tireless inspector a simple French boiled dinner, *Pot au Feu* or "Pot in the Fire," recreated with all its authentic time honored flare. Or perhaps, when he has a final insight into the case, Dupin might care to dine more festively on *Chicken Edgar with Truffles Swimming in a Rich Wine Sauce*, complemented by *Crème Fraiche aux Fruit*.

> *No wonder our wonder boy fails! What scene could create more unnerving unrest? Ellery and Inspector Queen match wits with their villain in a crowded department store on the last shopping day before Christmas.*

It is a *Pastrami Sandwich*, resplendent with a dill pickle, which Ellery brandishes sword-like, as he retells his triumph. We have recreated his, New York Deli style, and added some traditional sides dishes, such as *Kasha Varnishka* and *Cheese Knish*. Our *Turkey Stuffing* is likely to please Inspector Queen, although his exact recipe is a closely guarded family secret.

> *A group of friends meets regularly for dinner, serving up tales of crime with their capons. The supper party is replete with pompous writers, stuffy experts, and enough vanity and ego to fill Yankee Stadium. However, it is Asimov's unobtrusive and thoroughly deferential waiter Henry who regularly delivers the coupe de grace.*

Tonight let us enjoy the white-gloved service of the nonpareil Henry as he serves us *Iridescent Turtle Soup with Sherry on the Side, Veal Marengo in an Orange-Brandy Sauce, and Black Forest Torte Besotted with Kirsch*.

Martha Grimes

A Pub Crawl with Melrose Plant

A sheet of meringues, lightweight and sweet, sits in the oven, but Aunt Chris is nowhere to be found. Her nephew Johnny enlists Melrose Plant to help him find this vanishing lady. Their search takes them to forlorn rocky outcroppings, a past tainted by pornography, snuff films, and innocent children drowning in the cold sea.

Let's whip up some delightful *Meringues with Strawberries and Sabayon Custard,* just like Aunt Chris used to make. But don't taste them before you whet your appetite with *Roquefort-Baked Avocados,* and dine on *Cod* "that might have leapt from the water into the pan" *Smothered in Cucumber Sauce.*

Tony Hillerman

Navajo "Sole" Food

The body is in pretty bad shape. The soles of the feet are cut away. And the hands too. What's left of the body, "mostly a tattered ragbag of bare bone, sinew, gristle, and a little hard muscle" is rotten. It's enough to make Sgt. Jim Chee of the Navajo Tribal Police lose his appetite.

We have conspired to cook up something extra tasty for our favorite tribal policeman. Can we entice him to wrap his dry lips around moist and meaty *Navajo Kneel Down Bread, Hopi Venison Stew, Navajo Blue Hominy Posole, and Peach Crisp with Pinon Nuts?*

Introduction

Come, Watson, come. The game's afoot.

W ho hasn't secretly longed to heed the summons and go with Holmes into Victorian London's foggy night air, vanishing into a waiting carriage, the snap of the whip and echoing hoof beats piercing the darkness? Well, now it's possible. You can enter the world of your favorite detective and sit down with him or her for a quiet supper. Or morning tea, a Sunday picnic – even an old fashioned pub-crawl.

Appetite for Murder: A Mystery Lover's Cookbook takes readers on a culinary tour of classic crime fiction with the likes of Sir Arthur Conan Doyle, Agatha Christie, Edgar Allan Poe, and even Tony Hillerman. Each series of recipes features a particular detective and opens with an atmospheric vignette that evokes memories and sweeps the reader up into a favorite mystery all over again. Readers relive the tales of favorite sleuths and then turn their hands to creating the fare that solved the crime or caught the culprit.

In some cases the choice of cuisine actually plays a role in the crime or its solution. A dreadful poisoning launches "A Trifle Dangerous: a Luscious but Lethal Dessert with Miss Marple," while the curried mutton in "The Adventure of Silver Blaze" provides Holmes with the solution to the crime.

Other recipes are the fare of murderer or sleuth. Isaac Asimov and his fellow Black Widowers dine upon succulent veal Marengo, iridescent turtle soup, and sinfully rich black forest cake as they rack their brains to uncover unsolved crimes.

In a few instances, although there's no specific menu in the story, I've created one that fits the atmosphere. In this third recipe type there is considerable room for improvisation and creativity. We enjoy "French Country Fare and Fowl" with Poe's Inspector Dupin, feasting upon steaming *Pot au Feu* and rich *Crème Fraiche*.

I treat the mystery authors and their detectives with admiration but not awe. Their foibles are duly noted, laughed over, and warmly accepted like the eccentricities of a favorite uncle. We love Holmes even more for his misanthropic arrogance, Poirot for his preening vanity, and Rumpole for his stoic endurance of "she who must be obeyed."

Crime and cooking are old friends. What makes *Appetite for Murder* unique is that it draws upon the classic and popular detective fiction found on nearly everyone's bookshelf. What better introduced me to the magnificence of fine port and Albert Campion to the majesty of High Tea. I even enjoyed slumming with Horace Rumpole as he drank the cheap red wine he fondly called Pommeroy's plonk.

All these strange longings led to a work of love that found me thumbing through my favorites tales not for the crimes but for the crumpets. And I must admit that my favorite, Sherlock Holmes, with his ascetic ways, was not an easy mark. One only had to look at his skeletal frame to know that neither clotted cream nor fish and chips were on his menu.

Currently I enjoy giving Mystery Cooking classes featuring many of the recipes found in this book. Pictured here is a poster from a class at the Central Market Cooking School in Austin, Texas. "A Dinner to Die For" recreated the best of some infamous last suppers from Sir Arthur Conan Doyle, Agatha Christie, and Margery Allingham. Of course, we were careful to leave out the arsenic, foxglove leaves, and poison mushrooms.

Thus was born *Appetite for Murder: A Mystery Lover's Cookbook.* Because the mysteries that cradle these recipes are classic, the book's subject matter is timeless. And I have taken the traditional recipes and tweaked them with nouveau flair, so the old is suddenly new. It is my aim that this cookbook become a classic in itself and remain a mystery lover's companion for years to come.

THE GAME'S AFOOT

A Hearty Hunter's Supper with Holmes and Watson

"The Adventure of the Noble Bachelor"

Cooking is like love.
It should be entered into with abandon
or not at all.

Harriet Van Horne

Like many of the big events in history, it all begins with a wedding. We're not talking the golden apple and Trojan War here, but a "singular occurrence at a fashionable wedding," namely the sudden disappearance of the bride.

A jealous ex-lover disrupts the bridal luncheon, the newly wed American heiress abruptly disappears, and there are rumors of foul play. Lord St. Simon, the very noble yet penniless bachelor, has been left in the lurch.

This perky little melodrama gives us one of Holmes' most timely solutions. "I think that I shall have a whisky and soda, and a cigar after all this cross-questioning," he says. "I had formed my conclusions as to the case before our client came into the room."

And such a fine study in contrasts – stuffy old England and our persnickety groom set against wild, free America and the impetuous bride. Doyle never gets our dialect quite right, though, and his Americans invariably sound like reruns of *The Beverly Hillbillies*. All the talk of "claim jumping, falling down and doing a faint," and this or that being "dreadful hard" begins to pall after a while.

The noble bachelor is a dandy to end all dandies. The son of a duke, both Plantagenet and Tudor blood run in his icy veins He might be a bit upset about the disappearance of his bride and her accompanying purse strings, but the penniless lord dresses to the nines. What with his high collar, black frock coat, white waistcoat, yellow gloves, patent-leather shoes, and light-colored gaiters, he is Mr. GQ of Victorian England.

But why are the penniless ones always so pompous? While Lord St. Simon understands that Holmes has already managed several delicate cases, he thinks his visit to our detective has to take the cake, class wise. Not one to suffer fools gladly, Holmes replies with his typical wit. "No, I am descending. My last client was the King of Scandinavia."

St. Simon takes the put down in stride. Not much can shatter his ego. In fact, he is so sure of his matrimonial magnetism that he can only fathom that his bride had become suddenly deranged. How else could she abandon such a hunk? And this early, too – during the wedding breakfast!

Which makes our man Holmes sit up in his chair.

> They often vanish before the ceremony, and occasionally during the honeymoon;
> but I cannot call to mind anything quite so prompt as this. Prey let me have the details.

While Police Lieutentant Lestrade gets soaked dragging the Trafalgar–square fountain in search of Lady St. Simon's body, Holmes sits back in his chair and enjoys a good cigar. He does have to leave the comfort of hearth and home for a mysterious four hours but orders some take out our food delivered to 221 Baker Street. Well, not exactly your typical take out -- perhaps a bit classier than pizza delivery. I mean, when you are about to unveil another example of your brilliance to a command performance of all the relevant parties, you might as well set the stage with a little pizzazz. "A quite Epicurean little cold supper was laid out upon the humble lodging-house mahogany. There were a brace of cold woodcock, a pheasant, a *pate de foie gras* pie, with a group of ancient and cobwebby bottles."

Now maybe you'd like to join us while Holmes once again makes fools of about everyone involved in the case. Slide the linen napkin discreetly onto your lap, pick up the sterling fork, and try to look intelligent. We've spun the Victorian fare into the twentieth century and added a little haute cuisine of our own, courtesy of Executive Chef Roger Mollett of the award winning Central Market Cooking School. He's also providing a few words on appropriate wine selection, something just right to fit into those "ancient and cobwebby bottles."

Our menu includes *Grilled Quail Salad with Tarragon Citrus Vinaigrette*, (Cold woodcock is soooo hard to find today), *Brandied Pate de Foie Gras Pie, Smothered Pheasant in Sherry Cream Sauce, Pan Seared Venison with Wild Mushrooms and Chili Glaze,* and *Wild Rice and Pecan Pilaf.*

The saucier is a soloist in the orchestra of a great kitchen.

Fernand Point

Grilled Quail Salad with Tarragon Citrus Vinaigrette

Vinaigrette

1 teaspoon minced garlic
1 tablespoon Dijon mustard
2 tablespoons lemon juice
2 tablespoons minced fresh tarragon
3 tablespoons nonfat yogurt
1 tablespoon extra virgin olive oil
1/2 teaspoon sugar
 Salt and pepper to taste

Combine all ingredients in a blender or food processor. Pulse until thoroughly blended. Season to taste with salt and pepper

Salad

1 large gold bell pepper, roasted and peeled
1 small head of Boston lettuce
1 cups arugula leaves
2 large mushroom caps
2 large quail, split lengthwise
Cooking spray
Salt and pepper

Place a heavy (preferably cast iron) pan over medium heat. Seed and julienne the bell pepper. Rinse Boston lettuce; reserve four large lettuce leaves. Tear remaining lettuce into bite-sized pieces and place in a mixing bowl. Thoroughly rinse and dry arugula. (If not available, spinach leaves may be substituted.) Tear into bite-sized pieces and add to bowl with lettuce.

Spray mushroom caps and quail with cooking spray. Sprinkle with a little salt and pepper. Place mushroom caps and quail in hot skillet. Cook 3-4 minutes. Turn once and continue cooking until mushrooms are softened and quail in cooked through. Remove from pan, slice mushrooms and cut quail in half.

Place lettuce leaves on individual salad plates. Add 1/2 of the dressing to the lettuce / arrugula mixture and toss to coat. Divide between plates. Arrange julienned peppers, quail, and mushrooms on top of lettuce. Drizzle salad with remaining dressing.

Serve immediately.

Brandied Foie de Gras Pie

1 cup (1/2 pound) chicken livers
1/2 cup butter
1 medium onion, finely chopped
1 clove garlic, crushed
* Small bouquet garni
Black pepper, freshly ground
1 tablespoon brandy
4 to 6 tart sized pre-baked pastry shells
4 to 6 slices sharp cheddar or 6 ounces cream cheese
Freshly cut dill

In a skillet heat 2 tablespoons butter, and fry the onion with the garlic until just beginning to brown. Add the chicken livers, bouquet garni, salt and black pepper, and fry briskly for 3 minutes or until the livers are browned but still pink in the center. Cool, discard the bouquet garni and finely chop mixture or work it in a blender with a little of the remaining butter. Work the mixture through a sieve to remove the liver ducts. Cream the remaining butter and work it into the liver mixture. Add the brandy and taste for seasoning.

Spoon into pastry shells. Cover with a slice of cheddar cheese shaped to fit, or spread a thin layer of cream cheese on top. Garnish with freshly cut dill.

Chill for several hours.

*Bouquet Garni

Lay 3 sprigs of parsley, 2 sprigs of thyme, and 1 bay leaf in a 6" square of cheesecloth. Gather up the edges and tie into a bundle with kitchen string.

Smothered Pheasant in Sherry Cream Sauce

1 large or 2 small pheasants
1/2 cup flour seasoned with 1/2 cup freshly snipped herbs such as rosemary,
tarragon, and parsley
1/3 cup olive oil
1 cup chopped green onions
1 tablespoon minced garlic
1 cup sliced mushrooms or 2 medium truffles, sliced
1/2 cup cooking sherry
4 ounces nonfat sour cream

Clean bird; cut up. Roll in seasoned flour. In Dutch oven, brown pieces slowly on both sides in the olive oil, turning once. Drain away oil. Top with the onions, minced garlic, sliced mushrooms and 1/4 cup cooking sherry. Cover tightly and simmer at low heat 1/2 hour. Add sour cream and another 1/4 cup sherry to taste. (You can use 1/4 cup Madeira here if you want to be fancy.) Cover and simmer until tender--approximately 20 minutes

Pan Seared Venison with Wild Mushrooms and Chili Glaze

Sauce

1 cups beef or veal stock
2 tablespoons minced shallots
4 ounces brandy
4 tablespoons catsup
1 tablespoon chili flakes
1/4 teaspoon Tabasco sauce

Place stock in a heavy saucepan. Over medium heat, reduce by 1/2. Add remaining ingredients, return to a boil, reduce by 1/2. Place ingredients in a blender and puree until smooth. Set aside.

Steaks

1 large tart apple, cored
Cooking spray
2 teaspoons unsalted butter
1/2 cup wild mushrooms, chopped
1 tablespoon mined garlic
1 teaspoon minced green onion
1 pound venison tenderloin
4 teaspoons nonfat yogurt

Preheat oven to 375 degrees. Slice apple into 8 thin slices. Spray a nonstick sauté pan with cooking spray. Melt 1 teaspoon butter over medium heat. Sauté apples until lightly browned on both sides. Set aside. Melt remaining butter in pan. Add wild mushrooms, garlic, and green onion. Sauté until tender (approximately 2 minutes.) Remove from pan and set aside.

Return pan to stove; increase heat to high. Lightly salt and pepper venison tenderloin. When pan is very hot, place tenderloin in pan and sear all sides until browned. Place pan in preheated oven for 6-8 minutes, or until cooked to taste. Remove venison from oven and allow to set several minutes. Slice venison (on the bias) into 8 equal slices. Place 2 slices apple on each heated plate. Arrange 2 slices venison on apples. Drizzle venison with sauce; top with mushroom mixture. Top each with a spoonful of yogurt.

Serve immediately.

Wild Rice and Pecan Pilaf

1/2 cup chopped pecans
2 tablespoons unsalted butter, melted
1/2 teaspoon dried thyme, crumbled
1/4 teaspoon salt
Olive oil spray
1 medium onion peeled and julienned
2 tablespoons minced garlic
1 medium red bell pepper, julienned
1 1/4 cups wild rice, rinsed
2 1/2 cups nonfat chicken broth (or more if needed)
salt and pepper to taste

Preheat oven to 375 degrees. Combine pecans, melted butter, thyme, and 1/4 teaspoon salt in a baking dish. Mix well. Place in center of oven; toast 10 minutes or until crisp. Set aside

Spray a heavy 2-quart saucepan with olive oil spray. Place over medium heat. Add onion, garlic, and bell pepper. Sauté 5-7 minutes, or until slightly browned. Transfer to a bowl; set aside.

Spray pan with additional cooking spray; return to medium heat. Add rice, cook for 2-3 minutes, stirring constantly. Add chicken broth, bring to a boil, then reduce heat to medium low and cover. Simmer 40 minutes (or until rice is tender), stirring occasionally and adding additional stock if needed. Stir in onion and pecan mixtures, mix well, and transfer to an oven proof baking dish. Place dish in preheated 375 degree oven and bake 10 minutes. Season to taste with additional salt and freshly ground pepper. Serve hot.

This hearty meal deserves a wine that is hearty without being too heavy. A good Bordeaux will complement the robust flavors of the game and wine sauces without competing with them. Or choose from one of the drier varieties, such as Pinot Noir, Cabernet, or Merlot.

A WILD GOOSECHASE

Strange Birds and Bedfellows

"The Adventure of the Blue Carbuncle"

There never was such a goose.
It was sufficient dinner for the whole family...the youngest
Cratchits in particular were steeped in sage and onion to the
eyebrows.

Charles Dickens

J ewels have been hidden in some strange places by both nervous owners and fleeing thieves. Perhaps the strangest niche for a stolen jewel, however, is described by Conan Doyle.

In "The Adventure of the Blue Carbuncle" we find our purloined gem tucked away in a very seasonal pocket -- the crop of "a most unimpeachable Christmas goose." What endears us to this strangely named tale, after our initial relief that it isn't about a great purple festering boil, are the three main characters, a very seedy and disreputable felt hat, our most unimpeachable Christmas goose, and a scintillating blue stone. For even though the goose is quite dead, it and its two costars assume a life of their own in this Conan Doyle tale.

Though it is shot through with humans who alternately rant, cower, gasp, and faint, these seem only props for the ultimate drama – the life and loves of hat, goose, and jewel. We open with our king of detectives lounging on a sofa dressed appropriately in a royal purple dressing gown as he illuminates some points "not entirely devoid of interest" about the hat. Is it in earnest or merely a cruel taunt when he lends Watson his lens and asks him to ponder the habits of the missing owner of such? Of course, our poor Watson fails miserably and tells Holmes he can see nothing.

How tragic if Holmes had lived today, when a police lab could lift a few hairs from battered felt and run a DNA match with 99.999999% probability. The poor detective would probably wind up in drug rehab if he'd been fated to live into our twenty-first century.

To Holmes the life history of the hat's owner is "of course obvious." Oh, how we love it when he demeans us with his casual superiority. It is here that we, the more sadistic of Doyle's readers sometimes long for the occasional visit of Mycroft, Holmes' older and smarter brother, to set the upstart on his head, showing these great deductive leaps from felt to fortune, hats to husbandry to be mere balderdash. But alas, and to our secret satisfaction, Holmes seldom if ever receives his rightful comeuppance.

As he explains his reasoning to Watson with an ease which marks all great thinkers, Holmes' ideas are so clearly simple and logical that we smugly fool ourselves that we could, given a bit more time, have come to the same conclusions.

What has seemed only an intellectual exercise until now, finding the rightful owner of the battered hat, who had lost it and his Christmas goose in a street tussle with a band of roughs, takes a more sinister tone as Peterson, the commissionaire, enters. The ever- ripening fowl has gone to Peterson and his family to "fulfill the ultimate destiny of a goose," as Holmes so delicately puts it. But in its crop, his wife has found something extraordinary, "a brilliantly scintillating blue stone, rather smaller than a bean in size, but of such purity and radiance that it twinkled like an electric point." Holmes immediately recognizes the Countess of Morcar's blue carbuncle and recounts its cursed and sordid life:

> In spite of its youth, it has already a sinister history. There have been two murders, a vitriol-throwing, a suicide, and several robberies brought about for the sake of this forty-grain weight of crystallised charcoal.

Holmes and Watson must then leave the warm crackling fire of 221 B Baker Street and go out into the bitter night where "the stars were shining coldly in a cloudless sky, and the breath of passersby blew out into smoke like so many pistol shots." Footfalls ring out and the tension builds with the staccato beat of sharp sounds that punctuate the darkness like shattered crystal falling from an ice palace.

In hot pursuit of the goose's recent adventures, Watson and Holmes remind us of a pair of anxious parents tracking down the suspect friends of their rebellious teenager. At last, Holmes finds the culprit, and who can forget this sniveling little "shrimp" of a man with the cringing manner of Renfeild, Dracula's vampire in training. You remember, the one who couldn't even work up the gumption to suck human blood but smacked his lips over the dungeon spider population. Holmes doles out a lecture rather than Her Majesty's justice to the groveling thief and sends him away.

Reaching for his clay pipe before his half apologetic explanation to Watson, Holmes almost shrugs, "I am not retained by the police to supply their deficiencies." And they touch the bell to call forth Mrs. Hudson and their own dinner of roasted fowl. We can almost see Mrs. Hudson smoothing down her apron and pushing back a stray hair as she places the covered dish before her two favorite boarders.

Or perhaps, we are more comfortable in the cozy kitchen of Commissionaire Peterson, where he warms his feet in front of the open fire, pipe in hand as he chats with his wife. She nods and smiles as she deftly turns the white feathered goose into delectable country fare. We see her busy hands chop and dice and can almost smell the sweet herbs she has assembled for a stuffing. Now we sit in anticipation with this fine pair as we watch it brown ever so slowly over the open hearth.

Here is but one way "to fulfill the ultimate destiny of a goose." Our menu includes *Roast Christmas Goose with Apricot-Port Glaze, Cracked Wheat and Apricot Stuffing, New Potatoes in a Lemon Chive Sauce, Cold Asparagus in Walnut Drizzle, and Watercress Fennel Salad with Tarragon-Rosemary Vinaigrette.*

Judging from a remark of the Emperor Augustus –
that a certain task should be "done quicker than you could cook
asparagus" –
the Romans liked their asparagus barely blanched.

Mimi Sheraton

Roast Christmas Goose with Apricot-Port Glaze

1 10-pound goose
1/2 cup butter
Salt and pepper
1 recipe cracked wheat and apricot stuffing
1 onion, quartered
1 1/2 cups beef broth
12 peach halves (canned)
2 tbsps cognac
2 tbsps orange liqueur

Singe and wipe the goose. Rub inside of goose with 2 tablespoons butter, softened. Season with salt and pepper. Fill neck and body cavity with stuffing. Fold neck skin over and secure with small skewer. Sew up body cavity, truss bird, prick skin all over with a fork. Spread with 1 tablespoon butter, softened, and butter roasting pan with 1 tablespoon butter. Place bird in pan with onion. Roast in preheated 400 oven for 30 minutes. Pour off fat, season with salt and pepper, and pour on port wine from soaked fruit in stuffing. Lower heat to 350 and roast... basting 3 or 4 times, for 1 1/2 hours or until legs move freely in their sockets. Keep bird warm. Remove fat from roasting pan, pour in beef broth, and simmer for 5 minutes on top of stove, scraping the pan of all brown particles. Meanwhile, melt remaining 4 tablespoons butter and sauté well-drained peach halves until golden. Carve goose; arrange peach halves around it. Add cognac and liqueur to sauce and simmer for 5 minutes. Serve in a sauceboat.

Cracked Wheat and Apricot Stuffing

1 pound dried apricots, pitted
1 cup tawny port wine
2 cups cracked wheat (bulghur)
1/4 cup butter
2 medium onions, chopped
2 celery stalks, finely diced

1 tsp dried sage
Salt and pepper
1/2 pound dried prunes,
            pitted and halved
1//3 cup pine nuts
1 cup beef broth

Soak the apricots in the port overnight. Reserve port to baste bird. Soak the cracked wheat in 4 cups water for 2 hours. Drain well. Melt the butter and fry the onion and celery, add the well-drained cracked wheat and sauté for 5 minutes. Season with sage and salt and pepper to taste. Mix in prunes, pine nuts, drained apricots, and broth and simmer for 20 minutes.

New Potatoes in a Lemon Chive Sauce

12 (about 1 1/2 pounds) small new potatoes
1/3 cup butter or margarine
2 tablespoons minced chives
1 tablespoon lemon juice
2 teaspoons grated lemon peel
1 teaspoon salt
1/8 teaspoon pepper

Scrub or scrape potatoes and cook in boiling salted water for about 20 minutes or until potatoes are tender. Melt butter or margarine in a small saucepan. Stir in minced chives, lemon juice, lemon peel, salt and pepper. Drain potatoes and pour lemon-chive sauce over, turning to coat well.

Cold Asparagus in Walnut Drizzle

1 1/2 pounds fresh tender asparagus tips
1 cup finely chopped walnuts
1 to 2 tablespoons walnut or sesame oil
1/4 cup cider vinegar
1/4 cup soy sauce
1/3 cup sugar
Pepper

Cook asparagus in boiling water, covered, for 6 to 7 minutes or until just tender. Drain well and arrange in a serving dish. Mix remaining ingredients and pour over asparagus, lifting it so dressing penetrates. Sprinkle with pepper. Serve slightly chilled.

Watercress Fennel Salad with Tarragon-Rosemary Vinaigrette

The slight licorice tang of the fennel teams up with tarragon to give this salad a sweet piquancy.

1 bunch watercress
1 bunch fennel, thinly sliced
1 clove garlic, minced
6 to 8 scallions, minced
4 shallots, minced
2 leeks, thinly sliced

1 sprig fresh rosemary
Several tender tips fresh tarragon
Salt and coarsely ground black pepper, to taste
9 tablespoons olive oil

1 1/2 teaspoons Dijon mustard
4 tablespoons red wine vinegar

Mix first 6 ingredients in a large salad bowl. Discard any woody parts of the rosemary stem and chop with the tarragon. Sprinkle over salad. Drizzle the olive oil over the salad and toss thoroughly to coat. Salt and pepper to taste.

Blend mustard and vinegar, stirring with a fork. Drizzle over salad and toss again.

OFF TO THE RACES

Indian Spice and Everything Nice

"The Adventure of Silver Blaze"

Woe to the cook whose sauce has no sting.

Chaucer

W hat makes "The Adventure of Silver Blaze" so much fun, besides containing Holmes' arguably most famous line, is that it contains almost all the classic Conan Doyle elements.

The tale opens with our moody detective – not unlike a sullen rock star – recovering from one of his recurrent brooding fits with the necessary "rambling about the room, with his chin upon his chest and his brows knitted, charging and re-charging his pipe with the strongest black tobacco." Not so long-lived as those of our narcissistic divas, the restless pacing comes abruptly to an end as Holmes dons his famous deerstalker cap for the inevitable train ride through the countryside. .

Huddled in the first class carriage – we can almost hear the clacking of the rails and feel the steady vibration of the train - Holmes leans forward with his sharp and eager face to explain the facts of the case to Watson - the disappearance of the Wessex Cup favorite, Silver Blaze, and the mysterious death of its trainer, John Straker. The rhythmic clatter of hooves as Holmes and Watson rattle through quaint Devonshire towns marks the final leg of their journey.

Details are fleshed out with typical Victorian melodrama amid an atmosphere of Gothic gore. The trainer had lived in the lonely countryside surrounded by the complete wilderness of the moors. It is peopled only by the roaming gypsies encamped near the forlorn murder scene. On the night in question a maid carries the dinner of curried mutton to the stable boy on guard, her lantern light piercing the dark path across the open moor. A man appears out the darkness, his face "pale and nervous in the yellow light." The next day trainer John Straker's coat is found "flapping from a furze bush" that leads to the fatal hollow where they find the unfortunate trainer shattered by a savage blow. The right hand still holds a small knife "clotted with blood up to the handle."

But Gothic gore alone does not satiate the Holmes addict. We are not happy unless there is also considerable mucking about and groveling on the ground for clues, punctuated with the appropriate Holmes ejaculations.

"Halloa! What's this?" Holmes utters, stretched out upon the trampled mud of the crime scene. He finds the remnants of a half-burned candle but is not content until he has "clambered up to the rim of the hollow and crawled about among the ferns and bushes."

The only hint of his not unsubstantial ego in the piece is Holmes' acknowledgement of the Colonel's cavalier manner toward him and the prediction of future "amusement at his expense."

And amusement he does have, with his adroit unmasking of the culprit carried off with the finesse and legerdemain of the most clever magicians. This unmasking begins with the enigmatic reference to "the curious incident of the dog in the night-time."

Who can forget the following events which then unfold at a rapid pace. The mystery bay horse that wins the Wessex Cup is revealed to be the Colonel's beloved Silver Blaze, but only when "his face and legs are washed in spirits of wine."

Holmes utters what may be his most famous line as he explains to his readers, in the unlikely case that we, too, might have doubted him. "I had grasped the significance of the silence of the dog." Of course, we tell ourselves, the dog would have barked at an intruder. Here was the undeniable evidence of an inside job.

And now, finally, our food comes in, for everything centers upon the curried mutton. What better ingredient than pungent curry to disguise the "not disagreeable but certainly perceptible flavour" of the powdered opium used to drug the stable boy.

***

Because of Britain's strong ties to that country, Indian spice is a staple in the world of Holmes and Watson. It is, after all, at the fatal battle of Maiwand, shortly after arriving in Bombay, that young army surgeon John H. Watson receives a bullet in the shoulder. In his convalescent state he is returned to London and decides to share "some nice rooms" with "a Sherlock Holmes, an enthusiast in some branches of science."

Indian cuisine, with its special blend of exotic spices, remains a staple in Britain today. In fact, it has almost replaced the inevitable fish and chips as the preferred fast food in now cosmopolitan London.

Let us inhale its piquant sweetness as we anticipate our feast of Anglo-Indian delicacies. Our Kasmiri Griddle Lamb Kabobs are perhaps a bit more tender and refined than the curried mutton carried out to the stable boy by the little maid. And we can do without the powdered opium and depend upon our clear conscience to guarantee us a good night's sleep afterward.

Thanks to Suneeta Vaswani, a native of Bombay and now one of our country's foremost experts on Indian cooking, our menu bubbles over with seventeen exotic spices. In addition to the *Kasmiri Griddle Kabobs*, it features *Vegetable Pulao, Broccoli with Peanuts, Ginger, and Indian Spices; Prawn Balchow, and Grape Raita with Cilantro, Mint, and Green Chile Spiked with Yogurt*

The curry was like a performance of Beethoven's Ninth Symphony.
It stunned, it made one fear great art.

Anthony Burgess

Kasmiri Griddle Kabobs

1 pound ground lamb or beef
1 teaspoon salt 1/2 cup channa dal, rinsed and drained (looks like a yellow
 split pea, a smaller form of garbanzo bean)
2 teaspoons coriander seeds
3 black cardamoms, seeds only
12 cloves
20 peppercorns
1 teaspoon cayenne
1 cup pureed onion (2 medium)
Oil for pan frying

Combine meat and salt in a saucepan. Add enough water to cover and bring to a boil. Skim off the top. Lower heat to medium and cook uncovered, until water is absorbed. Drain any accumulated fat and cool slightly. Transfer to processor and pulse 4-5 times.

In the meantime, toast channa dal, coriander, cardamom seeds and cloves separately. Grind dal into a powder in a spice grinder. Divide powder in 2 batches. Combine coriander and cardamon seeds, cloves, and peppercorns and grind into a powder. Add to 1 batch of powdered dal. Stir in cayenne. Add powedered spices to meat.

Add pureed onions to meat and process to a paste. Transfer to a shallow container and chill uncovered about 2 hours. Just before cooking, mix reserved dal powder well into mixture. Adjust salt.

Heat 1 teaspoon oil in skillet. Taking 1 tablespoon of the mixture at a time, form small patties and brown in a skillet. Flip to brown other side. Handle patties carefully as they are fragile. Continue until all mixture is used. Serve with a chutney of your choice.

Vegetable Pulao
Traditional Indian Rice with Vegetables

2 cups Basmati rice
Oil for deep frying
1 cup cauliflower florets
1/2 cup potatoes, cut in 1/2inch cubes
1/2 cup carrots, cut in 1/2 inch pieces
1/2 cup peas
1 teaspoon black cumin (shah jeera)
2 bay leaves
4 inch stick cinnamon
1/2 teaspoon turmeric
Salt to taste

Wash rice in several rinses of cold water. When water runs fairly clear, leave in bowl, covered with 2 inches water. Soak 15 minutes.

Heat oil in a wok or pan for deep frying. When oil is fairly hot, fry cauliflower, potatoes, and carrots separately for 2-3 minutes each. Vegetables should be crisp. Remove and drain on a paper towel.

On a 4 quart saucepan, over medium heat, add 3 tablespoons hot oil. Fry black cumin, bay leaves, and cinnamon for 1 minute. Add drained rice, mix well, and sauté 2-3 minutes. Add vegetables, including peas, turmeric, salt and cold water -- about 3/4 inch above the level of the rice. Add salt. Cover and bring to a boil on high heat. Immediately reduce heat to low and cook covered 25 minutes. (Do not lift lid.) Check for doneness and turn off heat. Fluff lightly with a fork, replace lid slightly ajar and rest 5 minutes.

Again fluff with a fork and gently spoon onto a serving platter to serve.

Broccoli with Peanuts, Ginger, and Indian Spices

2 tablespoons oil
2 teaspoons cumin seeds
1/2 teaspoon fenugreek seeds
1/4 teaspoon asafetida
2 dry red chilies
3 cups chopped onion
2 tablespoons peeled and minced ginger
3-4 minced green chilies
1 tablespoon coriander powder
3/4 teaspoon turmeric
1 teaspoon cayenne
8 cups small broccoli florets
Salt to taste
1/4 cup roasted peanuts, coarsely chopped

Heat oil in a large wok or skillet. Add cumin seeds and sauté 1 minute. Add fenugreek, asafetida and red chili. Stir-fry 30 seconds to flavor the oil. Add onions and stir-fry until golden, about 6 -8 minutes. Add ginger and chilies. Cook 1 minute and add coriander, turmeric, and cayenne powders. Lower heat slightly and cook about 2 minutes.

Add broccoli and salt and mix well. Cover and cook on low heat until tender. Stir in peanuts and remove from heat. Serve with Indian bread.

Prawn Balchow

A kind of spicy pickle, this is not a side dish, but an accompaniment, eaten in very small quantities with each mouthful.

1 pound shrimp (prawns)
3/4 teaspoon cumin seeds
3/4 teaspoon peppercorns
5 whole dry red chilies
1 1/2 teaspoons turmeric
1 cup pure mustard or canola oil
2 cups chopped onions
8-10 fresh curry leaves
6 large Roma tomatoes, cut in quarters
6 large cloves garlic, partially smashed
2 1/2 by 2 inch piece peeled ginger, coarsely julienned
3 green chilies, preferably serranos, cut in 1/2 inch pieces
3 teaspoons salt
Additional cayenne to taste (optional)

Peel and devein shrimp. Wash and wipe dry. Process, pulsing 3-4 times, to coarse grind. Set aside. Grind cumin seed, peppercorns and red chilies to a fine powder. Mix with turmeric and set aside.

Heat oil and fry onions until golden. Add powdered spices and shrimp and fry 2 minutes. Add curry leaves and fry 1 more minute. Add tomatoes, garlic, ginger, green chilies, and salt. Simmer, uncovered until tomatoes are soft and the *masala* (mixture) looks well mixed, about 6-8 minutes. Add additional cayenne if desired.

Cool and bottle. This pickle can be refrigerated for up to 3 months.

Grape Raita with Cilantro, Mint, and Green Chile Spiked with Yogurt

4 cups plain nonfat yogurt
1 1/2 cups seedless grapes
1/2 cup cilantro leaves
1/3 cup mint leaves
2-3 green chilies, preferably serranos
Salt to taste

Stir yogurt until creamy. Stir in grapes. Make a smooth paste of cilantro and mint leaves and chilies. Add to yogurt. Add salt. Chill well before serving.

MECCA FOR MISANTHROPES

Dinner at the Diogenes Club with Mycroft Holmes

"The Adventure of the Greek Interpreter"

Oh, the pleasure of eating my dinner alone!

Charles Lamb

A giggling villain with cold, steel-grey eyes. A damsel in distress held captive in a dark, deserted house, her brother slowly starving to death for his refusal to sign away the family fortune. What a stew of melodramatic moments!

But the real fun of "The Adventure of the Greek Interpreter" is getting to meet Sherlock Holmes' smarter brother. Perhaps Watson has begun to worry that his readers will soon regard Holmes as he does, "an isolated phenomenon, a brain without a heart." It's time to come home and meet the family.

What we get is not exactly a warm and fuzzy bio tale indulged in by political consultants. There are not any photos of young Sherlock cradled in his mother's lap sitting atop the family pony. And brother Mycroft's digs are not exactly a cozy country retreat.

Most of the time, or more precisely, "from a quarter to five till twenty to eight" Mycroft can be found at the Diogenes Club, "the queerest club in London." Refuge for the most unsociable and most unclubbable men in town, its rules are both rigid and fiercely enforced. No member is allowed to take notice of another, and talking is not permitted, save in the Strangers' Room. Three offenses and the talker is expelled. You will never hear the equivalent of "How about dem Bears?" within its rarified walls. These guys aren't looking for companionship or someone with whom to share the latest cricket scores.

Holmes, who states that he cannot agree with those who rank modesty among the virtues, nevertheless acknowledges that "Mycroft has better powers of observation than I." Smarter he may be, but he is also Lazy with a capital L. An Odysseus lost in the land of the lotus eaters, Mycroft threads his way from his rooms in Pall Mall, round the corner to Whitehall, where he earns his daily bread by auditing government books, and over to the Club, just across the way. No other exercise.

No ambition, no energy. The true armchair, detective, he will not even go out of his way to verify his proposed solutions. He would rather be considered wrong than take the trouble to prove himself right.

Not just Holmes' smarter brother, also his fatter brother. The tactful Watson uses polite words, such as large, stout, or corpulent. He cannot help himself, though, after the first handshake, describing his encounter with "a broad, fat hand, like the flipper of a seal."

The case emerges now, a dark tale sketched out with broad strokes. Mr. Melas is Mycroft's fellow lodger. Of Greek extraction, he makes his living as an interpreter in the law courts. Two evenings earlier he has been visited by a very fashionably dressed young man who seems desperate for his services. Melas is whisked away in a waiting cab and held virtual prisoner by the gentleman, who rests a "most formidable-looking bludgeon" on the seat beside him. At a dimly lit country home he meets the giggling villain and two virtual prisoners. One is a tall and graceful lady in white, the other, Kratides, her older brother, who is being systematically starved to death.

The case takes on more urgency when the Brothers Holmes and Watson stop off to pick up Melas only to find that he has more or less been abducted again by the giggling ruffian with the cold, cruel eyes.

They arrive at the country house to find it dark and deserted. Holmes declares the nest empty, the birds flown. But not all the birds. A low, moaning sound is emanating from the second floor. As the men get closer, it changes from a dull mumble to a shrill whine. Holmes rushes the door and comes out choking. A dull blue flame of charcoal burns on a small brass tripod, and even the rescuers gasp and choke at its "horrible, poisonous exhalation."

A window is broken and they are able to retrieve the two men crouched against the wall. They are "blue lipped and insensible, with swollen, congested faces and protruding eyes." Alas, Mr. Kratides, the damsel's older brother, has succumbed to the evil vapors, but the always restorative brandy with a chaser of ammonia is administered to Melas by the able Dr. Watson, whose hand draws him "back from the dark valley in which all paths meet."

We are left with little other satisfaction save the piecing together of the tale. A purely mercenary marriage for the damsel in white had been futilely contested by her martyred brother. The two culprits had fled with the girl a virtual prisoner. But a curious piece in a newspaper from Buda-Pesth finishes the tale with a final twist.

> It told of how two Englishmen who had been traveling with a woman had met with a tragic end. They had each been stabbed, it seems, and the Hungarian police were of opinion that they had quarreled and had inflicted mortal injuries upon each other. Holmes, however, is, I fancy, of a different way of thinking, and he holds to this day that if one could find the Grecian girl one might learn how the wrongs of herself and her brother came to be avenged.

Not a complete victory, to be sure, but at least one giving some reassurance that the Victorian sense of order is still in place.

Let us assume that Holmes and Watson steal over to share the strange news clipping with Mycroft and Melas. What better way to celebrate the vanquishing of those two perpetrators of evil than dinner at the Diogenes Club. If we were allowed within its sacred doors, our meal would be prepared to meet the exacting standards of its demanding and eccentric members. And, of course, this elegant repast would be served by the most discreet and unobtrusive of waiters, embellished by candlelight, old silver, and fine china. But, shhh. Remember, no talking allowed.

We will feast upon *Golden Rissoles with a Port Cumberland Sauce, Mushrooms in Sherry Cream, Carrottes a la Flamande, and Blanc Mange in Custard Sauce.*

*It is the duty of a good sauce
to insinuate itself and imperceptibly awaken the palate.*

Grimod de La Reyniere

Golden Rissoles

1 recipe Fritter Batter made
      with sugar, white wine, and
      a few drops almond extract
1 pound pork, beef, or veal
      shoulder ground
1/2 teaspoon dried thyme
1/8 teaspoon black pepper
1/4 teaspoon powdered allspice
1/8 teaspoon nutmeg
1/4 teaspoon powdered ginger
1/2 teaspoon dried sage
4 eggs, separated
Corn or peanut oil for frying

Prepare fritter batter. Mix pork thoroughly with salt, pepper, allspice, nutmeg, ginger, sage, and thyme. Beat egg whites until stiff and mix gently into meat. Beat yolks lightly and reserve. Heat oil to 360. Shape meatballs about the size of limes and drop a few at a time into oil. Deep fry for 8 to 10 minutes or until balls float on surface and are firm. Drain on paper toweling until they are as dry as possible. Coat with batter and refry at 375 for 3 to 5 minutes or until they are light golden but not brown. Drain well and thread onto skewers. If skewers are large, several balls can go on each but leave 1 1/2 inches between them. Dab well on all sides with thick coating of egg yolk. Broil in a preheated broiler, turning frequently so that all sides become golden. Dab on more egg yolk if necessary. Remove from skewers and serve plain or with Cumberland Sauce.

Fritter Batter

1/2 cup flat beer
2/3 cups flour, sifted
1 whole egg
1/8 teaspoon salt
1 egg white

Beat the beer, flour, and whole egg until smooth. Let stand for 30 minutes. Add salt to egg white and beat until stiff. Fold into batter. For Golden Rissoles, white wine may be substituted for beer and 2 teaspoons of sugar and a few drops of almond extract may be added.

Cumberland Sauce

Rind and juice of 1 orange
Rind and juice of 1/2 lemon
4 shallots, minced
1/3 cup currant jelly, melted
1 cup port wine
1 teaspoon prepared mustard
1/4 to 1/2 teaspoon powdered ginger
Cayenne pepper

Cut rinds in julienne strips and simmer in water for 15 minutes. Drain well. Simmer the shallots in water separately until tender. Drain and press out any moisture. Add orange and lemon rind and shallots to currant jelly. Add wine and strained orange and lemon juice. Dilute mustard with a little sauce and stir in. Season with ginger and cayenne pepper to taste. Serve cold.

Mushrooms in Sherry Cream

1 1/2 pounds mushrooms, sliced or quartered,
        or whole button mushrooms
1 medium onion, finely chopped
1/3 cup butter
1 cup heavy dream, heated
2 cups sour cream, heated
2 tablespoons dry sherry
2 to 3 tablespoons chopped, fresh dill
Salt and freshly ground pepper

Wash mushrooms. Peel if necessary and remove woody part of stems. Slice or quarter. Brown mushrooms with the onion in hot melted butter in a large, heavy frying pan. Add the sweet and the sour cream and simmer very gently, stirring continually until very hot and smooth. Add sherry and dill. Salt and pepper to taste. Serve immediately.

Carrottes a la Flamande

12 young carrots, sliced
Salt
Fried bread triangles
4 tablespoons butter
1 cup beef broth
Pinch of sugar
2 tablespoons chopped parsley

Parboil the carrots in salted water for 5 minutes. Drain well. Melt 2 tablespoons butter in a saucepan; add the carrots, beef broth, and sugar. Cover and simmer until well cooked. Reduce the broth to practically nothing and add the remaining butter and parsley. Serve surrounded with little triangles of fried bread (optional).

Blanc Mange (White Food)

1 cup finely ground blanched almonds
2 1/2 cups heavy cream
3/4 cup sugar
2 envelopes unflavored gelatin
1 teaspoon rose water (optional)
1 teaspoon almond extract
3 egg whites, stiffly beaten
1/8 teaspoon salt

Pour 1 1/2 cups cold water over almonds and let them stand for 2 to 3 hours. Strain through a cloth, pressing hard on almonds to extract all possible liquid. Reserve almond "milk," discard the nuts. Scald the cream with the sugar, stirring until sugar is melted. Soak the gelatin in 1/2 cup cold water, dissolve in the hot cream, then cool. Flavor with rose water and almond extract and combine with the almond milk. When the mixture begins to set, fold in the egg whites with the salt. Pour into a 2-quart buttered ring mold and chill until set. Unmold. Fill with berries; serve with almond-flavored Custard Sauce.

Custard Sauce

3 egg yolks
1/3 cup sugar
Pinch of salt
1/2 cups light cream
1 teaspoon rose water
1 teaspoon vanilla or almond extract (or 1 teaspoon of rum, brandy, sherry,
        or dry white wine)

Beat the yolk of egg, sugar, and salt until very light in color. Scald the cream and pour into the eggs, stirring briskly. Pour into the top of a double boiler placed over 1-inch barely simmering water. Cook, stirring until mixture coats the spoon, about 7 to 8 minutes. Cool, stirring occasionally; flavor with rose water and vanilla extract and chill.

Lederhosen and Legerdemain

An Alpine Affair with Pastry Light as Air

"The Adventure of the Final Solution"

I raised to my lips a spoonful of the cake.
A shudder ran through my body.

Marcel Proust

E nough of this lounging about in a purple dressing gown. Forget about filling the pipe with tobacco gleaned from the Persian slipper above the fireplace. And no more tedious interviews with pasty-faced housemaids or sniveling petty thieves. In "The Adventure of the Final Solution" we have an action-filled battle with a worthy adversary, and Holmes is the prey rather than the unruffled predator.

"I have been a little pressed of late," he tells Watson. Edging his way around Watson's consulting room to fling shut and bolt the shutters, Holmes describes the day's events.

He has nearly been trampled by a horse carriage, just missed a falling brick which shatters to fragments at his feet, and been attacked by a bludgeon-wielding rough. And the source of all this, a man who pervades London but has never been heard of. Not a nameless thug, but a man of good birth and excellent education is this slight mathematics Professor Moriarty.

Holmes teeters between awe and disgust for this antagonist who is at last his equal. He is the "Napoleon of crime, a genius, a philosopher, an abstract thinker."

Their face-to-face encounter is one between two who know each other so well that all superficial conversation is rendered useless. Moriarty stands upon Holmes' threshold, almost a daguerreotype of our detective.

> He is extremely tall and thin, his forehead domes out in a white curve, and his two eyes are deeply sunken in his head. He is clean-shaven, pale, and ascetic-looking, retaining something of the professor in his features. His shoulders are rounded from much study, and his face protrudes forward, and is forever slowly oscillating from side to side in a curiously reptilian fashion.

It's almost as though these two have a Vulcan mind meld.

"All that I have to say has already crossed your mind."

"Then possibly my answer has crossed yours."

Honestly, we begin to believe that Moriarty is wasting his time with the personal visit. The two are already communicating almost telepathically. It all ends with some mumbling about "standing clear" versus "standing fast" and an ominous threat of being "trodden under foot."

Of course, we are prepared for some hard times by Watson's not too subtle opening.

> It is with a heavy heart that I take up my pen to write these the last words in which I shall ever record the singular gifts by which my friend Mr. Sherlock Holmes was distinguished.

Even we less alert readers suspect more than a severe case of writer's block.

The net that Holmes has woven round his Nemesis is set to close in just three days time, but Holms needs safe haven until it happens. So now our relentless hunter becomes the hunted and he must use all his wits save his skin.

The chase begins with all the standard gumshoe ways to dodge a tail so Watson can get to Victoria Station where he will rendezvous with Holmes.

Watson performs with breathless obedience, but instead of meeting Holmes, sees only a "venerable Italian priest" who speaks but broken English. Suddenly the aged ecclesiastic turns his face, the wrinkles disappear, the nose reasserts itself, the lower lip is drawn in, and the eyes regain their fire. No cheap, pull off the latex ala Tom Cruz in *Mission Impossible*, but a true impersonation gained more by acting and body language than accoutrements.

Once again, as we are treated to Holmes' penchant for disguises, we are not quite sure if it is his genius or Watson's naiveté that allows his best friend to be amazed at each unmasking.

But dealing with an adversary on his intellectual plane requires continued zeal. They safely elude Moriarty for the requisite three days, but then a telegraph message informs Holmes that the police have secured all the gang except its leader. Aware of "the shadow which lay across him," as he and Watson tramp through the beautiful Alpine villages of Switzerland, Holmes reminisces about his life with somewhat maudlin and immodest musings.

> I think that I may go so far as to say, Watson, that I have not lived wholly in vain. If my record were closed to-night I could still survey it with equanimity. The air of London is the sweeter for my presence.

Here, astute readers may detect Doyle's motives for wanting to kill off this egotist who had seized life from his pen, and like an endlessly bowing baritone, would not leave the stage.

Doyle does provide a perfectly frightful setting for the demise of his creation, though. Reichenbach Falls is a fearful place.

> The torrent, swollen by the melting snow, plunges into a tremendous abyss, from which the spray rolls up like the smoke from a burning house.

We smell a rat in the request for Watson's presence to "oversea a fellow countrywoman dying in a strange land," but true to his colors, our intrepid narrator is a dupe till the end. He returns from this obvious ruse to find a short note from Holmes wherein he describes the final death struggle between the two relentless foes.

So ends Watson's final tribute to one "whom I shall ever regard as the best and the wisest man whom I have ever known."

But how, choking back our tears, could we possibly have a taste for Swiss pastries at such a time? Well, he isn't dead, of course. Doyle's attempt at murder ran afoul of the pack of avid fans that refused to let their pet detective leave them. Bowing to their pressure, he resurrected Holmes some ten years later in "The Adventure of the Empty House."

So now that our appetite has returned, let's indulge in some of that delightful Swiss pastry you've been promised. Imagine yourself in the little village of Meiringen, where Holmes and Watson are fellow guests at the Swiss Inn, *Englischer Hof*. You are surrounded by the mountain air, gentle green slopes, and buxom waitresses in skimpy lederhosen. Sit back and enjoy every bit of this decadence. But don't be lured away by any urgent telegrams.

Let's indulge in *Tarte Bourbonnaise, Birnennwecken Pear Cake from the Berne District with Pears, Prunes and Figs Soaked in Wine, Fondue Brillat-Savarin with Sliced White Truffles, Drunken Strawberries Featuring a Fruity Young Pinot Noir,* and *Tarte Suisse with Pine Nuts and Fresh Swiss Chard.*

A gourmet who thinks of calories is like a tart who looks at her watch.

James Beard

Tarte Bourbonnaise

While the French claim the quiche originated in Lorraine and the Germans in Alsace, the diplomatic Swiss make no claims, but only bake and enjoy its delicious lightness.

1 1/2 recipes short pastry
2 cups light cream
1 egg yolk
1 teaspoon flour
4 whole eggs
1/2 teaspoon salt, or to taste
Cayenne pepper

1/2 teaspoon powdered nutmeg
1 cup Gruyere cheese
2 tablespoons butter

Roll out the pastry and line a pie plate or a 9-inch pan ring placed on a cookie sheet. Prick with a fork; chill thoroughly. Line with foil and fill with rice or dried beans to keep shell from puffing. Bake for 10 minutes in preheated 425 oven. Discard foil and rice and cool. Scald cream and cool. Beat egg yolk with flour, beat in eggs, add cream, and beat until smooth. Season to taste with salt, pepper, and nutmeg. Sprinkle tart shill with cheese, pour in custard, dot with butter, and bake in a preheated 375 degree oven on bottom shelf for about 40 minutes.

Short Pastry

1 1/2 cups flour
1 teaspoon salt
1/4 cup vegetable fat or lard
5 tablespoons ice water
butter as needed

Resift flour and salt into a bowl. Using knives or a pastry blender, cut in butter and fat until it looks like coarse meal. Add ice water by the tablespoon until pastry just holds together. Roll out 1/8 inch thick.

Birnennwecken Pear Cake from the Berne District with Pears, Prunes, and Figs Soaked in Wine

2 pounds dried pears
1/2 pound prunes
1/2 pound figs
1 cup dry red wine
1 tablespoon butter
1 1/2 cups chopped walnuts
1 cup coarsely chopped raisins
2 tablespoonss each:
       minced candied orange peel
       lemon peel
       citron
1 cup sugar
2 tablespoons powdered cinnamon
1 tablespoon powdered cloves
1/3 cup kirsch
3 tablespoons lemon juice
quadruple short pastry recipe
1 egg yolk for glazing
vanilla sugar

Soak pears, prunes, and figs overnight in a mixture of wine and enough water to cover. Add butter and simmer in the wine for 40 minutes or until liquid evaporates and fruit is soft. Drain and cool. Remove pits from prunes and chop fruit coarscly. Add all remaining ingredients except pastry dough, egg yolk, and vanilla sugar, and mix thoroughly. This filling improves in flavor if it is left to ripen for 2 to 5 days in the refrigerator.

Prepare dough as directed and roll out to 4 to 6 rectangles, each about 5 inches wide and 9 to 10 inches long. Spoon a 1/2 inch thick strip of filling down the center of each dough rectangle, leaving 1 1/2 inch band of dough on each side. Wrap dough around filling and gently turn over onto lightly buttered and floured cookie sheet so the seam side of the dough is down. Pinch ends closed with a little cold water and flatten rolls slightly. Prick the dough in several places with a fork. Cut a few diagonal slashes on each roll and with a knife. If using yeast dough, let rise for 30 minutes. Brush dough with 1 egg yolk beaten with 2 tablespoons milk and bake in 375 oven for 30 or 45 minutes or until golden brown. Cut into 1 to 2-inch slices and serve warm or cold, sprinkled with vanilla sugar.

Vanilla Sugar

2 cups sugar
1 vanilla bean

Put sugar in a jar with vanilla bean; close tightly. Let stand for two days before using.

Fondue Brillat-Savarin with Sliced White Truffles

1 pound Gruyere or fontina cheese, grated
1 cup milk
4 tablespoons butter
4 egg yolks or 2 whole eggs, lightly beaten
A 3 1/2-ounce can white truffles, finely sliced (optional)
Freshly ground black pepper

Soak the cheese in the milk for 1/2 hour. Melt the butter in an earthenware casserole or chafing dish. Add the cheese, milk, and eggs. Stir with a wooden spoon over low heat until the cheese is melted and the mixture is creamy and smooth. Cover with a topping of thinly sliced white truffles and pepper. Serve over toast.

Drunken Strawberries Featuring a Fruity Young Pinot Noir

4 cups fresh, ripe strawberries
2-3 tablespoons sugar
fruity young pinot noir or beaujolais
*creme fraiche

Wash and trim 4 cups fresh, ripe strawberries. Cut into quarters. Sprinkle with sugar and toss. Set aside for about 45 minutes. Serve in large wine goblets with just enough wine to cover the fruit. Dollop with creme fraiche. for added elegance.

*Creme fraiche
Literally fresh cream, creme fraiche is a rich, heavy country cream with a tart flavor, similar to our dairy cream but richer and sweeter. The French use creme fraiche for many purposes, from thickening and enriching soups and sauces to garnishing desserts and pastries. This easy method of creating the cream enables you to produce a variety of fresh-fruit desserts in minutes. To create this simple version, combine 2/3 cup whipping cream with 1/3 cup dairy sour cream

Tarte Suisse with Pine Nuts and Fresh Swiss Chard

Pastry
2 cups flour
1/2 teaspoon salt
1/2 cup water
1/2 cup extra-virgin olive oil

Combine the flour and salt. Stir in the water and oil until blended. Knead mixture briefly and press into an 11'by 13' baking dish. Refrigerate.

Filling
2 tablespoons olive oil
1/2 cup minced green onions
1/2 pound Swiss chard leaves or other greens, stems removed, leaves
 washed and chopped
1/4 cup chopped fresh herbs, such as basil, fennel leaves, and dill
Coarsely ground black pepper
1/2 cup finely diced cooked ham
1/2 cup finely diced Gruyere cheese
2-3 tablespoons mayonnaise
1 teaspoon Dijon-style mustard
1/3 cup pine nuts
2 eggs, beaten

Sauté the onion in the olive oil until translucent. Add the chard and cook an additional 10 minutes. Season with freshly snipped herbs and coarsely ground black pepper.

Preheat oven to 375 degrees. Mix the remaining ingredients in a large bowl. Fold in the sautéed chard mixture. Scrape the mixture into the prepared tart shell. Bake 40 to 45 minutes or until the crust is golden and the filling firm. Let cool before serving.

A TRIFLE DANGEROUS

A Luscious but Lethal Dessert with Miss Marple

"The Tuesday Night Club"

The dessert is said to be to the dinner what the madrigal is to literature—
it is the light poetry of the kitchen.

George Ellwange

D on't ever underestimate them. The spinsters. Those white-haired little old ladies with the knitting needles and sweet smiles. They know what evil lurks in the heart of man.

Agatha Christie, the Grand Dame of mysteries, created a new prototype for sleuths in her Miss Marple. Unlike the focused, reclusive, and almost arrogant Holmes, Miss Marple is a meandering stream. She is sociable, unassuming, and so like our own doddering grandmother that her acute observations often go unnoticed.

No matter that she never married, that she hardly strays from her simple village of St. Mary Mead. People are people, whether in the sophisticated shops of London or in her homely village, and Miss Marple is an acute observer of human behavior. She knows that many a cold-blooded killer can be absolutely charming, that evil absolutely exists and must be stamped out. She might be knitting something white and soft and fleecy, but behind those clicking needles is someone every bit as resolute as Madame Lafarge.

Her black brocade dress with its cascade of mechlin lace down the bodice and her snowy hair hidden under a black lace cap create such a portrait of benign inconsequence that she is almost left out of the Tuesday Night Club's true crime quest by default.

The group is a gathering of professionals with egos to match. When Raymond West, Miss Marple's "self-consciously debonair" nephew announces unsolved mysteries, he blows out a cloud of smoke for dramatic effect. Of course he thinks he has the inside track on solutions. After all, a writer sees motives that the ordinary person would pass by. Presumably to writers, all others are "ordinary persons."

So too, that man of the world, Sir Henry Clithering, late Commissioner of Scotland Yard, refers to the others as laymen with the same half derisive label used by the clergy. Now the elderly clergyman of the gathering, Dr. Pender, puts in his bid, too. After all, the clergy hear things, you know; they "know a side of human nature which is sealed to the outside world."

Even the dried up solicitor, Mr. Petherick, who looks "over and not through his eyeglasses," makes his claim. The legal profession is able to sift through the facts, to look at things impartially, he insists.

Joyce Lempiere, the artist with "her close-cropped black head and queer hazel-green eyes," proclaims women's intuition and the artist's sensibility as her trump cards.

But one thing they can all agree on is Miss Marple's disqualifications. Joyce sweetly dismisses "darling Miss Marple." with a smile. How could she possibly know life, sequestered as she is in the quaint village of St. Mary Mead.

When she tries to explain the mystery of Mrs. Carruthers and her missing two gills of pickled shrimps, even the courtly Sir Henry calls it a fishy story. Raymond derides it as a "sort of village incident." Mr. Petherick's only response is his dry little cough.

No wonder Joyce almost doesn't even consider including Miss Marple in the proposed Tuesday gatherings until she gently inserts herself.

I think it would be very interesting, especially with so many clever gentlemen present. I am afraid I am not clever myself, but living all these years in St. Mary Mead does give one an insight into human nature.

Not the village thing again, they must all be silently groaning. Only cavalier Sir Henry musters up a courteous reply. He then takes the lead in describing an old case.

Three people sat down to a dinner of tinned lobster. All were taken ill, but only one died. At the time, death was considered due to ptomaine poisoning, and the victim was duly buried. Later an autopsy found the cause of death to be arsenic.

As he describes the actors in this little drama, Miss Marple sagely nods her head. She is readily familiar with these types:

> The good-looking, florid husband, a traveler for a firm of
> manufacturing chemists
> The rather commonplace middle-aged wife
> The professional companion, "a stout cheery woman of about sixty."
> The local doctor's daughter, a good- looking woman of thirty-three
> The meek little housemaid, Gladys Linch

And so it is Miss Marple who solves the case. With typical homespun logic and a cook's attention to detail, she focuses on another part of the menu. Not the lobster, but the dessert. She easily surmises the source of the arsenic –"the hundreds and thousands on the trifle dear. Those little pink and white sugar things." The dieting companion would ignore all sweets, and the murdering husband could easily scrape the candied decorations off his portion.

The fresh raspberries and sherry drizzle in our trifle recipe make this "inevitable English dessert" anything but. The arsenic, of course, is optional.

Recipes include not only the *English Trifle with Fresh Raspberries and Sherry Drizzle*, but also *Jammed Lemon Curd Tarts from the Derbyshire Market Town of Bakewell, Petticoat Tails, and Maid of Honour Tarts.*

For a gourmet wine is not a drink but a condiment.

Edouard DePomiane

English Trifle with Fresh Raspberries and Sherry Drizzle

1/2 cup sugar
3 tablespoons cornstarch
1/4 teaspoon salt
3 cups milk, or
3 egg yolks, beaten
3 tablespoons margarine or butter
2 teaspoons vanilla
1 teaspoon almond extract
1 package ladyfingers
2 tablespoons sherry
2 cups raspberries
1 cup chilled whipping cream
2 tablespoons sugar
2 tablespoons toasted, slivered almonds

Mix 1/2 cup sugar, the cornstarch, and salt in a 3-quart saucepan; gradually stir in milk. Heat to boiling over medium heat, stirring constantly; boil and stir 1 minute. Stir at least half of the hot mixture gradually into egg yolks. Stir back into hot mixture in saucepan. Boil and stir 1 minute. Remove from heat; stir in margarine, vanilla, and almond extract. Cover and refrigerate at least 3 hours.

Split ladyfingers lengthwise into halves. Layer half of the ladyfingers, cut sides up, in 2-quart glass serving bowl. Sprinkle with 1 tablespoon of the sherry. Layer half of the raspberries and half of the cold egg yolk mixture over ladyfingers; repeat. Cover and refrigerate at least 4 hours, but no longer than 8 hours.

Beat whipping cream and 2 tablespoons sugar in chilled bowl until stiff; spread over dessert. Sprinkle with almonds unless you favor arsenic-spiked candies.

Additional English Desserts:

Jammed Lemon Curd Tarts from a Derbyshire Market Town

1 cup flour
1 tablespoon margarine
1 tablespoon superfine sugar water
6 tablespoons jam

Put the flour into a large mixing bowl and rub in the margarine, using your fingertips, until the mixture resembles fine breadcrumbs. Stir in the sugar and add enough water to form a firm dough. Roll out on a lightly floured board and use to line an 8-inch pan dish. Spread the jam over the base and chill.

Lemon Curd Filling

2 egg yolks
1/2 cup sugar
1/2 cup butter, melted and cooled
Grated zest of 1 lemon
Juice of 2 lemons
2 egg whites, stiffly beaten

Beat the egg yolks; then beat them with the sugar until very light. Add the butter, lemon zest, and juice. Fold in egg whites. Pour over jam filling. Bake for 25 to 30 minutes in a preheated 350 degree oven until curd is set. Serve warm or cold.

Petticoat Tails

1 cup butter, softened   1/2 tsp baking powder
1/2 cup granulated or brown sugar   1 tsp vanilla extract
3 cups flour, sifted

Cream butter with sugar. Resift flour with baking powder and add to butter. Add vanilla. Press into 4
7-inch round pans and prick well all over with a fork. Press a small juice glass into the center of each pan to form a circular mark; then mark off eight wedges from circle to edge of each pan. Bake in a preheated 350 oven for about 20 minutes or until golden. Cool in pan. Gently cut markings and lift off. Almond extract or grated orange or lemon rind may be substituted for vanilla. Shortbreads may be decorated with multicolored sugar before baking or iced with thin sugar icing.

Maids of Honour Tarts

These little tartlets are said to have originated at the court of Henry VIII, when he chanced one day upon some of the Queen's maids of honour eating cakes. Being famous for his voracity, he could not resist the temptation to try one himself, and found them so delicious he named them Maids of Honour. Still another legend says Ann Boleyn, then a maid of honour, invented the tiny tarts to win the love of Henry VIII.

1 1/3 cups bakers' cheese
6 tablespoons softened butter
2 eggs
1 tablespoon brandy
2 tablespoons superfine sugar
1/4 cup ground almonds
Pinch of ground nutmeg
A few flaked almonds
8 ounces puff pastry, defrosted.

Roll the puff pastry out on a lightly floured board and use to line 12 lightly greased muffin-tin wells. Mix together all the remaining ingredients, except the flaked almonds, and spoon into the pastry cases. Sprinkle a few flaked almonds on each and then bake at 425 for 15-20 minutes until the pastry is golden brown and the filling is set.

SEEDS OF DECEPTION

Succulent Duckling Stuffed to Death

"The Herb of Death"

To the Chinese the duck,
because of its affection for his mate,
represents marital fidelity.

Mimi Sheraton

Being a popular writer is a little like being a good-looking actor. No one takes you seriously. We love her plots, twists, characters, and easy readability so much we don't even notice Agatha Christie's skill. Like all experts, she makes it seem so easy.

Look at the names. There's a Dickenesque aptness. Sure, she's not as eloquent as the bard, and I don't recall any sonnets she penned, but Agatha Christie's understanding of human nature is every bit as shrewd. And what about a story within a story? Like Chaucer, we learn about the teller of the tale by how he tells it. As we revisit this little saga, look for Dickens, Shakespeare and Chaucer hiding in the wings.

A garden and seeds of evil sown there one fine spring day. Foxglove seeds sown among the sage so that a mistake should be made when the cook assembled the stuffing -- a fatal mistake for one Miss Sylvia Keene.

We return to another Tuesday Night Club true crime mystery, this time with a little different group. The teller of the tale is Mrs. Bantry, the slightly loopy neighbor of Miss Jane Marple. On the surface she seems the conventional upper class wife, spending her days tending to the servants and complaining about the difficulties of getting good scullery maids. She likes men and flowers, though not necessarily in that order, and refers affectionately to her husband, Colonel Bantry, as an old duffer.

There's the beautiful young actress, Jane Helier, who thinks a garden would be nice, "that is, if you hadn't got to dig or to get you hands messed up." Dr. Lloyd gives the group some medical knowledge, especially about digitalis, the active ingredient in foxglove. Our two repeats are Sir Henry Clithering, formerly of Scotland Yard, and Miss Jane Marple with her "gently quizzical blue eyes."

Though Sir Henry calls her Scheherazade, Mrs. Bantry is no natural storyteller. "You're quite good at the facts, Dolly, but poor at the embroidery," the colonel teases. Mrs. Bantry insists she knows no stories and obstinately shakes her head. Her eyes wander, and her mind strays to the latest bulb catalogue.

Seizing upon that opening, Sir Henry gently prompts her. "The garden. Can't we take that as a starting point? Come, Mrs. B. The poisoned bulb, the deadly daffodils, the herb of death!"

A chord is struck. There is story at last, but Mrs. Bantry's recital of it is bare bones to the extreme.

> One day, by mistake, a lot of foxglove leaves were picked with the sage. The ducks for dinner that night were stuffed with it and everyone was very ill, and one poor girl – Sir Ambrose's ward – died of it.

The group finally lands upon a game of twenty questions to put some flesh on those bones, although Mrs. B (Don't call her that to her face. It's not dignified.) finds that choice of words offensive.

"Don't speak so ghoulishly," she scolds. "And don't use the word flesh. Vegetarians always do. They say, 'I never eat flesh,' in such a way that puts you right off your nice little beefsteak."

The cast of characters emerges, each with Mrs. B's unique spin. Sir Ambrose is distinguished, charming, courtly even, with beautiful white hair, but very delicate with a weak heart. His ward, Sylvia Keene is very pretty, fair-haired with lovely skin, but in fact, rather stupid. Her companion is one of those middle-aged women who always seen to dig themselves in comfortably somewhere, "one of those widows left in unfortunate circumstances, with plenty of aristocratic relations, but no ready cash." Mr. Curle is as musty as the old parchment on the rare books he discusses, and as his name suggests, an elderly stooping man. Jerry Lorimer, the boy next store engaged to Sylvia, seems exactly that. And finally, Sylvia's friend, Maude Wye, is "one of those dark, ugly girls who manage to make an effect somehow."

Everyone has his go and several possibilities emerge. Once again the male professionals, the medical man and Scotland Yard expert, seem so logical and focused. Dr. Lloyd focuses on the erratic nature of poisons in their raw state. One couldn't be sure which one would die from the foxglove. Perhaps Sir Ambrose, since he already had a heart problem, was the intended victim. The smooth talking companion is mentioned in his will and she'd decided to take an early retirement. Sir Henry opts for Maude Wye. It was the old love triangle, according to him. After all, Miss Wye and the ward's fiancé, not exactly the boy next store, we now learn, had been seen kissing on the terrace before dinner.

Jane, ever beautiful but not particularly original, follows the good doctor's lead. Sir Ambrose was the intended victim, but the victim herself, Sylvia, was the would-be killer. The old man had been sticking out against her marriage to Mr. Wonderful next store, and now she'd get her hands on youth and money at once. Too bad she succumbed to her own tricks. Perhaps Mrs. B was right. Sylvia wasn't too bright.

But Jane Marple is not listening. She is somewhere far else. St Mary Mead, of course, thinking of old Mr. Badger, the chemist, secretly married to his young housekeeper. When Mrs. B chides her with the slightly insulting, "Now then, school marm," Miss Marple reveals the real solution laughing beneath the shadows of impeccable male logic.

You already know the answer, too, don't you?

Then rest your brains and sit down with us for *Roast Wild Duck with Orange Gravy Stuffed with Fresh Sage, Rosemary, and Lemon Thyme.* The recipe is considerably improved without the addition of deadly foxglove leaves.

Rosemary:
If you carry a stick or fragment of this shrub,
no evil spirit can come near you.

The Physicians of Myddfai (13th Century)

Roast Wild Duck with Orange Gravy

2 wild ducks
1/4 cup butter
Salt and pepper
3-4 slices bacon
Flour for sprinkling
Watercress for garnish

Gravy

3-4 strips orange rind
Juice of 1 orange
1 tablespoon butter
1 small onion, sliced
1 cup well-flavored stock
1/4 cup port or red wine
Pinch of cayenne
Black pepper, freshly ground
Trussing needle and string
1 teaspoon arrowroot mixed to a paste with 1 tablespoon water (optional)

Fresh Sage, Rosemary, and Lemon Thyme Stuffing

3 cups toasted whole grain bread cubes
2 cups finely diced celery
1 tablespoon grated orange peel
3/4 cup diced orange sections
1 tablespoon each, finely chopped
  fresh garden sage
  fresh rosemary
  fresh lemon thyme
1/3 cup snipped parsley
3/4 teaspoon salt
dash coarsely ground pepper
3 tablespoons wild rice
1 beaten egg
1/4 cup melted butter or margarine

Toss together bread, celery, orange peel, diced orange section, fresh herbs, seasoning, and wild rice. Combine egg and butter; add to bread mixture, tossing lightly.

Preparation

Set oven at 350 degrees. Put 1 tablespoon butter, mixed with salt and pepper, inside each duck. Stuff lightly and truss them. Lay bacon slices over the breasts. Heat remaining butter in the roasting pan, put in ducks, and baste with hot butter.

Roast ducks in heated oven, basting frequently, for 1 1/2 hours or until they are tender. Just before the end of cooking, remove bacon slices from the ducks, sprinkle the breasts with flour, baste well, and cook 5 minutes longer.

For gravy: In a pan heat butter and fry the onion until golden. Add the orange rind and stock; simmer 10 minutes and strain. Return liquid to the pan; add the strained orange juice, port or wine, cayenne, salt and black pepper. Bring to a boil and, if you like, stir in a little arrowroot paste to thicken the mixture slightly. Transfer to gravy boat.

Remove the trussing strings from ducks and gently spoon out the stuffing. Transfer ducks to a warm platter, and garnish with watercress. The stuffing may be placed on same platter or in a separate serving dish.

MORNING MUSINGS WITH MISS MARPLE

Treacle Tart at St. Mary Mead

"The Idol House of Astarte"
"The Blue Geranium"
"A Christmas Tragedy"

*Love and scandal are the best
sweeteners of tea.*

Henry Fielding

While the traditional hour for high tea in Britain is 4 P.M., a more casual and homey custom is to have "elevenses" one hour before noon, something akin to our American coffee break. I can think of no better place to enjoy this cozy affair than in the parlor of Miss Jane Marple in the quiet village of St. Mary Mead. Our treats would be served by Edna, Miss Marple's little maid, probably on simple Stadfordshire blue country crockery. Of course, the tea would be hot and strong, and the cream so thick that we would have to spoon it on our warm scones. Miss Marple, "rather pink and flustered," would be busy with her knitting, telling us about those curious inhabitants of St. Mary Mead.

"At Lady Shipley's garden party last year the man who was arranging the clock golf tripped over one of the numbers –quite unconscious he was – and didn't come around for a bout five minutes."

In between our noisy sips of the delightful brew we learn how this freak accident helped her solve the mystery so romantically called "The Idol House of Astarte" by the old clergyman, Dr. Pender.

All that mumbo jumbo about the spell of the Phoenician goddess possessing the beautiful Diana Ashley hadn't impressed her. Would we like another scone, by the way? Or what about one of those nice treacle tarts with custard sauce? Sir Richard had tripped over a tree root or something just as the man arranging the clock golf had. While he was passed out, his cousin had stabbed him. It was easy enough. He was in costume, dressed as a brigand and must surely have weapons on his body.

"I remember dancing with a man dressed as a brigand chief when I was a young girl. He had five kinds of knives and daggers, and I can't tell you how awkward and uncomfortable it was for his partner." Miss Marple's pink cheeks become more so.

***

She takes a sip from the fine china cup. Miss Marple remembers other uncomfortable clothes from her own years of nursing. Those starchy uniforms and the starchy proper behavior expected of those wearing them. One had to wear such uncomfortable collars, and often the job was a bit… delicate.

> We always had litmus paper for ---well, for testing. Not a very pleasant subject. That's how I knew about the blue geranium. If it had been yellow and not pink before, I might have been wrong.

The district nurse in St. Mary Mead had some problems of a delicate nature too. And she was pretty, just like young Nurse Copling in the Colonel's Blue Geranium story. Miss Marple wasn't drawn in by Madame Zarida's admonition: The Blue Primrose means Warning; the Blue Hollyhock means Danger; the Blue Geranium means Death…

It all had to do with the litmus paper and the smelling salts – the ammonia in the salts could turn the pink to blue.

***

Edna, the tidy little maid brings in a fresh tray of orange and walnut crumpets surrounded by steaming seed cakes. Miss Marple smiles her approval. Now Edna isn't perfect, sometimes even clumsy at times. But she is honest and good. Not like Ethel...

> Ethel was a very good-looking girl and obliging in every way. Now I realized as soon as I saw her that she was the same type as Annie Webb and poor Mrs. Bruitt's girl. If the opportunity arose, *mine and thine* would mean nothing to her.

Miss Marple could sense things about people. She was right about Ethel just as she was about Mr. Sanders. From the first moment she saw the Sanders together, she knew that he meant to do away with her. And when he "lost his balance" on that tram and fell right against his wife, she was sure he was rehearsing some sort of accident.

She looked away. "Sanders was hanged,"said Miss Marple crisply. "And a good job, too. I have never regretted my part in bringing that man to justice. I've no patience with modern humanitarian scruples about capital punishments."

"Would you like another scone?"

Let the scones be soft, but not your scruples. Help yourself to our Elevenses tray of sweets including *Treacle Tart with Custard Sauce, Orange and Walnut Crumpets, and Seed Cake Drenched in Cognac.*

To the ancient Greeks such delicacies as custards were suitable only for women and children.

Mimi Sheraton

Treacle Tart with Custard Sauce
Short Pastry

1 1/2 cups flour
1 teaspoon salt
1/4 cup vegetable fat or lard
5 tablespoons ice water
Butter as needed

Resift flour and salt into a bowl. Using knives or a pastry blender, cut in butter and fat until it looks like coarse meal. Add ice water by the tablespoon until pastry just holds together. Roll out 1/8 inch thick.

Tart
1 portion Short Pastry (See above)
2 cups bread crumbs or crushed cereal flakes
1/2 cup molasses mixed with 1/2 cup light corn syrup

Roll out pastry on a lightly floured board to about 11 inches in diameter. Press gently into 9-inch pie plate. Trim excess and use fork tines to shape edges. Spread crumbs or flakes evenly over crust. Then pour molasses syrup all over flakes. Use pastry trimmings to form narrow strips. Use these to make a latticework pattern over tart. Make in a preheated oven at 425 for 20 to 25 minutes. Serve with custard sauce or thick cream.

Custard Sauce

3 egg yolks
1/3 cup sugar
Pinch of salt
1/2 cups light cream
1 teaspoon rose water
1 teaspoon vanilla or almond extract (or 1 teaspoon of rum, brandy, sherry,
      or dry white wine)

Beat the yolk of egg, sugar, and salt until very light in color. Scald the cream and pour into the eggs, stirring briskly. Pour into the top of a double boiler placed over 1-inch barely simmering water. Cook, stirring until mixture coats the spoon, about 7 to 8 minutes. Cool, stirring occasionally; flavor with rose water and vanilla extract and chill.

Orange and Walnut Crumpets

Sometimes called piketlets, these griddle-fried cakes are similar to but somewhat softer than "English muffins."

2 cups water and milk, mixed
1 tbsp active dry yeast
4 1/2 cups bread flour
1 tsp salt
3 tablespoons grated orange rind
1 cup chopped walnuts

Heat the water and milk mixture until just tepid and remove from heat. Dissolve the yeast in a little of the warm liquid. Put the flour and salt into a large bowl, make a well in the center, and pour in the yeast and remaining liquid, mixing well with a wooden spoon. Add the grated rind and chopped walnuts and mix them well, but don't overbeat. Cover the bowls with plastic wrap, and keep in a warm place until the mixture rises.

Heat a lightly greased cast iron griddle and place the greased, metal crumpet or flan rings on top. Tuna cans with tops and bottoms removed are an excellent substitute. Spoon in some of the mixture, to about half way up the rings, and cook until bubbles form on the top, then remove the rings and cook for another couple of minutes, until the underside is lightly browned. Serve with butter and homemade jam.

Seed Cake Drenched in Cognac

Often called nun's cakes because baking them was one of the few leisure activities permitted medieval sisters, they continue to enjoy popularity in Britain. Along with tea and treacle tart, this confection is frequently mentioned in Agatha Christie's writing.

1 cup butter
1/2 cups sugar
6 egg yolks
3 egg whites
3 1/2 cups flour, sifted
1/4 teaspoon salt
3 teaspoons baking powder
3/4 cup milk
1 tablespoon caraway seeds
1 1/2 teaspoons vanilla extract
5 tablespoons cognac
Confectioner's sugar for dusting

Cream butter and sugar until light and fluffy. Add the egg yolks, beating well. Stir egg whites, breaking up just slightly, and add to mixture. Beat well for 1 minute. Resift flour, salt, and baking powder 3 times and fold into mixture gradually, alternating with the milk. Fold in caraway seeds and vanilla. Pour batter into buttered and floured 9-inch tube pan. Bake in a preheated 350 oven for 50 to 55 minutes or until toothpick comes out clean. Cool for 2 to 3 minutes, unmold, and invert to cool on a cake rack. Puncture the cake all over with a wooden skewer. Drench with cognac and allow to cool completely. Serve sprinkled with powdered sugar.

A HOLIDAY WITH HERCULE

Plum Pudding Prophecies

"The Adventure of the Christmas Pudding"

The English Puritans outlawed Plum Pudding as "sinfully rich."

Agatha Christie herself referred to this short story as "an indulgence of my own, since it recalls to me, very pleasurably the Christmases of my youth. The boys of the family and I used to vie with each as to who could eat most on Christmas Day." Some of the special treats Ms. Christie recalls from Abney Hall, the home of her brother-in-law's family in the north of England, are turkey, roast and boiled, sirloin of beef, plum pudding, mince-pies, trifle and an infinite supply of chocolates.

"**M**e—I am not an Englishman," says Hercule Poirot. "In my country, Christmas, it is for the children. The New Year, that is what we celebrate."

So runs the Belgian detective's warm response to an English Christmas in the country. The little man shutters at the thought of a fourteenth-century manor house with its draughts and poor plumbing.

Mr. Jesmond of the Home Office tries his best to appeal to Poirot's patriotism with the standard clichés, muttering about grave issues of state, matters of utmost delicacy and so on. But what really lures the bearer of those little grey cells is the newly installed oil-fired central heat, the splendid hot water system, and the worry that things might even be too warm.

All hinges on a ruby with a long trail of bloodshed and deaths behind it -- what self-respecting gem doesn't have a cache of corpses connected to it? The heir apparent of an unnamed monarchy -- we must be ever so discreet, you know -- has somehow misplaced his wedding necklace. Well, not misplaced exactly. In keeping with family tradition (his father bestowed Cadillacs on favorite dancing girls) the royal son has allowed his girl friend of the moment to wear the necklace "just for one evening." A quick trip to the powder room and she takes a powder.

The suspected thief is to be a guest at Kings Lacey, and the ever discreet Jesmond arranges for Poirot also to be a guest. Here we meet the charming Mrs. Lacey, still the coquette at nearly seventy, with girlish dimples in her wrinkled cheeks. She knows Desmond Lee-Wortley is absolutely no good, "but I can still feel his charm, all right."

Mrs. Lacey knows nothing about an indiscreet prince or a blood-tainted ruby, but she is concerned about her granddaughter Sarah's infatuation with a man of bad reputation.

With her shrewd assistance Poirot manages to unmask the thief of hearts and rubies, solving matters of love and politics in one fell swoop.

> I want you to be happy, Sarah. Ah, there's your young man bringing his car around. You know, I like those very tight trousers these young men wear nowadays. They look so smart -- only, of course, it does accentuate knock-knees.

Poirot's work begins with inquiries about the Christmas pudding. Mrs. Ross tells his that a good

Christmas pudding should be made some weeks before and allowed to wait. Another custom is for everyone to come into the kitchen and "have a stir and make a wish." When the day of feasting arrives, buried treasure is discovered in several portions -- a silver button predicts bachelorhood; a thimble, spinsterhood; a ring, marriage; a pig, gluttony, and a ten shilling gold piece, the prospect of money. The unexpected object is an enormous piece of red glass. Only Hercule Poirot dares suspect it to be the stolen ruby.

Finally, the jewel is safe and the scoundrel is hoisted on his own petard. Let us indulge in an old fashioned Christmas dinner of English exuberance, with not one, but two turkeys, if you like. We start with *Creamy Oyster Soup*, followed by *Oven Roasted Christmas Turkey* with *Chestnut Stuffing*. Ours is a special recipe from an Austrian chef bestowed on Mrs. Ross. And let's not forget to leave enough room for a *Homemade Mince Pie Steeped in Dark Rum and Cognac*, and, of course, *the Grand Plum Pudding.*

Mincing of meat in pies saveth the grinding of the teeth.

Sire Francis Bacon

Creamy Oyster Soup

2 to 4 tablespoons unsalted butter
2 tablespoons or minced green onions or leeks
1 clove garlic, minced
1/2 cup minced celery
1 to 1 1/2 pints shucked oysters, with their liquor
1 1/2 cups milk
1/2 cup light cream
1/2 teaspoon salt
Dash paprika
2 tablespoons snipped fresh parsley or dill

Set the top part of a double broiler directly over low-medium heat and combine the butter, onions, garlic, and celery. Cook for about 5 minutes, until the onion is tender and translucent, but not browned. Stir in the oysters, milk, cream and seasonings. Place the double boiler over, not in, boiling water and warm until the oysters float to the top. Garnish with fresh parsley or dill. (Makes about 4 cups.)

Homemade Mincemeat Pie Steeped in Dark Rum and Cognac

2 pounds beef neck
1 pound suet
4 pounds tart apples
4 cups sugar
2 pounds currants
3 pounds seedless raisins
1/2 pound citron, cut fine
Juice and grated peel of 2 oranges
Juice and grated peel of 2 lemons
1 1/2 cups cider
1 tablespoon salt
2 teaspoons powdered cinnamon
1 teaspoon each powdered mace, cloves, and nutmeg
1/4 cup dark rum
1/4 cup cognac

Simmer beef in water to cover until tender, about 3 hours. Cool, put through coarse blade of a food processor with suet and apples. Add other ingredients; mix. Simmer 1 hour.

Use 2 cups for an 8-inch pie. Fill pastry-lined pie pan and adjust to crust. Bake in a very hot oven (450 degrees) about 35 minutes.

Chestnut-Herb Stuffing

3 quarts slightly dry bread cubes
2 teaspoons each freshly snipped sage, thyme, and rosemary
1 1/2 teaspoons salt
1/3 cup snipped parsley
1/2 cup finely chopped onion
1 cup chopped celery
1 cup boiled chestnuts, chopped (*Save milk)
6 tablespoons butter or margarine, melted
1 cup condensed chicken broth
      * or 2 chicken bouillon cubes dissolved in chestnut milk and water to make one cup

Combine bread, seasonings, parsley, onion, and butter. Add broth and toss lightly to mix. Makes 8 cups, or enough stuffing for one 12-pound turkey.

Oven Roasted Christmas Turkey

Stuff and truss turkey just before roasting. Stuff wishbone cavity lightly; skewer neck skin to back. Tuck wing tips behind shoulder joints. Rub large cavity with salt. Spoon in stuffing. Shake bird to settle stuffing; do not pack.

Close opening by placing skewers across it and lacing shut with cord. Tie drumsticks securely to tail. (If opening has band of skin across, push drumsticks underneath; you won't need to fasten opening or tie legs.)

Grease skin thoroughly. Place breast side up on rack in shallow roasting pan and leave in this position for entire roasting time. Cove with loose "cap" of aluminum foil, pressing it lightly at drumstick and breast ends, but avoid having it touch top or sides. For a 12 pound turkey roast at 325 for approximately 4 1/4 hours.

Grand English Plum Pudding

1/2 cup all-purpose flour
1/2 tsp ground cinnamon
1/8 tsp ground nutmeg
1/8 tsp ground cloves
1/2 tsp baking soda
1/2 tsp salt
1 cup raisins
1/2 cup currants
1/4 cup candied fruit peel
1/4 cup cut-up candied cherries
1/4 cup chopped walnuts
3/4 cups soft bread crumbs
1 cup ground suet
1/2 cup packed brown sugar
2 beaten eggs
1 tablespoon brandy
1/4 cup brandy (optional)

Mix flour, spices, baking soda, and salt. Stir in fruit, walnuts, and bread crumbs. Mix suet, brown sugar, eggs, and 1 tablespoon brandy; stir into flour mixture. Pour into well-greased 4-cup mold; cover with aluminum foil.

Place mold on rack in Dutch oven; pour boiling water into Dutch oven to rack level. Cover and boil over low heat until wooden pick inserted in center comes out clean, about 3 hours.

Remove mold from Dutch oven; unmold. Heat 1/4 cup brandy until warm; ignite and pour over pudding. Serve with hard sauce.

Hard Sauce

1/2 cup sweet butter, softened
1 1/4 cups confectioners' sugar
1 egg white, slightly beaten
1 teaspoon vanilla extract or
        1 tablespoon cognac or rum

Cream the butter with the sugar and egg white until thick and fluffy. Flavor with vanilla, cognac, or rum. Chill well before using.

ABOARD THE ORIENT EXPRESS

Steam Whistles, Supper, and a Stabbing

Murder on the Orient Express

*After a good dinner, one can forgive anybody,
even one's own relations.*

Oscar Wilde

It's always better when it happens on a train. Whispered words of passion muffled by clacking wheels, narrow lovemaking in the upper berth, a grisly murder behind polished mahogany. Conan Doyle, Agatha Christie, and that grand master Alfred Hitchcock all knew that even the mediocre was infused with drama when it rode the rails.

And what train is imbued with more romance and mystique than the exquisite Orient Express, threading its ways through dessert, mountain, and mosque-clad sunsets on its trek from Istanbul to Paris?

Clouds of steam flood the station, a whistle wails through the thick air, and a white haired attendant calls "All aboard." Hercule Poirot, his mustache oiled and shaped, adjusts the carnation in his lapel and deftly steps over oily puddles to avoid soiling his spats. Just as the ancient steam engine departs, he steps aboard. Little does he suspect the grisly murder that will punctuate his journey.

Or perhaps he does. For when Poirot passes a "most respectable American gentleman,"

> I had a curious impression. It was as though a wild animal -- animal but savage! you understand -- had passed me by. The body -- the cage -- is everything of the most respectable -- but through the bars, the wild animal looks out.

When this same American asks Poirot to act as his bodyguard, he refuses, at first politely. "I regret that I cannot oblige you." Pushy insistence and promises of big money finally bring out a more frank reply.

"If you will forgive me for being personal -- I do no like your face, Mr. Rachett,"

Obviously there are others who share this opinion. They next day Rachett is found murdered in his bed with no less than twelve stab wounds.

But there are too many clues for Poirot. They are delivered, deposited, and literally drop down upon him -- the stopped watch in the dead man's pocket, a button from a conductor's tunic, a tunic with a missing button, and finally, a jeweled dagger with blood on it.

The passenger suspects are a varied lot. They are

> The American secretary to Rachett, long-headed and sober
> A swarthy Italian picking his teeth with gusto
> A neat Englishman with the expressionless face of a well-trained
> servant
> A big American in a loud suit
> The Russian princess with a yellow, toad-like face
> A woman with a long amiable face rather like a sheep
> A stout, elderly woman talking in a monotone with no signs of
> pausing
> An English governess, tall, slim, and coolly efficient

A Colonel from India, lean of figure, brown of skin
A lady's-maid with a broad, expressionless face.
A big man, well made, of the Hungarian Embassy
His chic wife with manicured hands and deep red nails

Only Poirot comes to know what unites all twelve. They are inextricably tied to a grisly murder in American, a sensational crime that took not one, but five lives.

Before Poirot calls them together to propose two entirely different solutions to the crime, he has time for an exquisite meal in the dining car, one that suits even his finicky tastes. Feast your eyes upon the polished silver trays, the crisp white linens, the gleaming crystal, and join him for an exquisite meal of *Sole Marguery in Wine Sauce, Spinach Crepes, Pommes de Terre Lyonnaise, and Apple Cream Steeped in a Lemon, Thyme and Rosemary Wine Sauce.*

*A special order beverage to accompany dessert for Poirot would be a steaming cup of chamomile tea, "a beverage of which he is inordinately fond," according to Hastings, or thick, sweet chocolate. He disdainfully refers to English coffee as "your English poison."

Crepes:

*One taste would reform a cannibal into
a civilized gentleman.*

Edward Prince of Wales

Sole Marguery in Wine Sauce

12 mussels
2 cups dry white wine
4 shallots or 1 small onion, chopped
4 large fillets of sole
Salt and pepper
4 tablespoons butter
3 tablespoons flour
12 cooked shrimps, shelled and deveined
2 egg yolks
1/2 cup heavy cream

Scrub and wash mussels, removing beard. Steam with 1/2 cup water in a covered pot until mussels open, about 5 minutes. Discard any mussels that remain closed. Shell mussels and remove black portions. Strain and reserve stock.

Put the wine and shallots in a wide skillet with a cover and simmer for 5 minutes. Place sole fillets in the wine, season with salt and pepper, cover, and simmer gently for 5 to 7 minutes or until fish slakes when tested with a fork. Remove fish with a slotted spatula to a heated serving platter.

Add stock from mussels to sole stock and simmer briskly for 5 minutes. Melt 3 tablespoons butter in a saucepan, add the flour, stir, and cook for 3 minutes. Add strained fish stock and stir until thickened. Simmer for 5 minutes. Add mussels and shrimps. Beat yolks into the cream; gradually add some sauce to cream and pour all back into saucepan on very low heat. Stir until smooth and thickened but do not boil. Remove from heat and swirl in remaining tablespoon of butter. Pour sauce over sole fillets.

Spinach Crepes

Crepes

2 eggs
1 cup flour
1cup milk

Make the crepe batter by beating the 2 eggs thoroughly. Then beat in the flour. Stir in 1 cup milk. Put the batter in the refrigerator to rest while you prepare the filling.

Filling

3 tablespoons butter
1 chopped onion
2 garlic cloves, minced
1 bunch fresh spinach, washed and dried and chopped, or 8 ounces frozen,
 thawed, drained, and chopped
4 eggs, hard-boiled and chopped
1 cup coarsely grated cheddar cheese

In a non-aluminum pan (aluminum tends to blacken spinach and/or make it taste bitter and acidy), melt butter. Gently sauté the onion, then add garlic and chopped spinach. If fresh spinach is used, cover for about 2 minutes to wilt it down. Turn off heat. Add chopped eggs and cheese.

Cream Sauce

3 tablespoons butter
3 tablespoons corn starch
1 1/2 cups milk
dash nutmeg
salt and pepper

Dissolve the cornstarch in 1/2 cup milk. Melt the butter or margarine in a stainless steel pan over medium heat. When it begins foaming, add the milk mixture, stirring continually. Add the rest of the milk, salt and pepper, nutmeg, and stir until the sauce comes to a boiling point. Lower the heat and continue stirring until the sauce thickens. The sauce is ready when it is smooth and thick.

To make thin crepes, oil or butter a 7-inch crepe pan. For each crepe, use about 7 tablespoons of the batter (as much as necessary to cover the bottom of the pan) and swirl around. Cook one side briefly until it turns light brown and then, with the help of a spatula, turn and cook the other side.

Place a spoonful of filling on each crepe, roll up and arrange in baking dish. Cover with cream sauce. Bake at 300 degrees for 15 minutes.

Pommes de Terre Lyonnaise

3 large onions, sliced
1/2 cup butter
6 firm medium potatoes, boiled, peeled and sliced
Salt and freshly ground pepper

Separate onions into rings and sauté in the hot butter until golden. Gently toss potatoes with onions until they are lightly browned. Season to taste.

Apple Cream Steeped in a Lemon, Thyme, and Rosemary Wine Sauce

6 apples, quartered
1 1/2 cups sugar
2 cups rose wine
Rind of 1 lemon
Pinch of dried rosemary
Pinch of dried thyme
1 envelope unflavored gelatin
1/2 cup sweet sherry
1 cup heavy cream, whipped

Place the apples in a pan with the sugar, rose wine, lemon rind, rosemary, and thyme. Simmer until apples are very soft. Strain and reserve wine. Puree the apples through a fine strainer into a bowl; add reserved wine. Soak gelatin in sherry for 5 minutes. Melt over hot water and add to apples. Stir well and cool. When the apple mixture begins to stiffen, fold in the cream. Pour into a mold that has been rinsed in cold water and chill in the refrigerator until firm. Unmold.

The Cask OF CANTONETTI

Albert Campion's Almost Last Supper at Savarini's

Death of a Ghost

Wine is bottled poetry.

Robert Louis Stevenson

Here's the deal. You're on to him. That unscrupulous art dealer who has cooked up one fantastic scam. And he knows it. You wonder just how Max Fustian is going to kill you.

He has already put two other people out of the way – yes, a bit crudely, but with such panache.

That first one took some cool nerves, right there in the middle of a crowded art show. And stylish, too. The scissors that gutted Tommy Dacre were a piece art in themselves. They had

> …slender blue blades some nine inches long and handles so encrusted
> with chunks of coral and cornelian that it seemed impossible they
> could ever be used.

How clever to have the murder occur just after his ex-fiancé has displayed signs of a jealous fit, but over such a small thing. Tommy finds the perfect model, a beautiful Italian girl who has "the dark, mournful eyes and arched brows of a Florentine Madonna." What with entry papers being so hard to come by, nowadays, it is the only thing he can do to get her into the country. Marry her, that is.

Even you, Albert Campion, are off your game. At first you only notice "some commotion on the far side of the room. " The doubled up figure has fainted, it seems. Then the true tragedy is revealed, and you fall into the laid trap and suspect Linda.

The second murder is better planned. What better way to knock off a nervous co-conspirator than to make her more nervous still, so she would turn to drink. But this time the drink is laced with nicotine, "one of the most pernickety poisons in the world."

Now this clever killer has invited you into his lair. The game is up and you both know it. He invites you to sample a homemade cocktail, shaking "a few drops of poisonous-looking green stuff from a bitters bottle in to a minute shaker." Then your guard shifts to the cherry, which he insists is an integral part of the concoction. He conveniently leaves the room and you notice a greyish white paste in place the cherry stone. Carefully you put it in your pocket.

The dinner at Savarini's has you a bit worried, too. The Cantonetti is brought out with much fan fair in a basket lined with vine leaves. The wine glasses are a full ten inches high, and the napkin which cradles the bottle is the size of a cot sheet. Max drinks to your health and you feel a bit like Poe's Fortunato.

Those delicious mushroom omelettes get you to thinking of fungus poisons. The crepes and tournedos, the "curious savoury mess of sweetbreads and chicken liver" are sampled through a growing warmth brought on the Cantonetti – that and the many gin cocktails you've been slurping up all afternoon. By the time the Danubian cheese course arrives you are feeling distinctly odd. Then that hazy gnat of a memory buzzing round what is left of your brain bites. The gin. Cantonetti is "the most marvelous stuff in the world," if you haven't had any alcohol within the last twenty-four hours. And if it's gin… "then, oh, my hat!"

You feel like a player in one of those Hitchcock affairs where you are surrounded by good, well-meaning folks who cannot help. You tell someone you are in danger and he laughs at the drunken clown "in danger, yes, of falling down." Max lurches against you and you fall over into the street where a nice policeman picks you up with a smile.

The homemade cocktail, the tainted cherry, the ominous omelette -- just scams to distract you from the simple but real danger. A plainly drunken man teetering on the train platform with the train "screaming now, nearer and nearer and nearer..."

Can we leave Campion teetering on the platform for just a little while? He hasn't done justice to that grand meal served to him at Savarini's. Let's nibble on *Mushroom Omelettes in Port Sauce, Tournedos Maconnaise, and Veal Sweetbreads in the Basque Style.*

A toast to the Cocktail Party
Where olives are speared
And friends are stabbed.

Anonymous

Mushroom Omelettes in Port Sauce

Sauteed Mushrooms
1 lb. any variety or combination of mushrooms, wiped clean and sliced
Flour to Coat Mushrooms
Enough olive oil to coat a large skillet
2 to 3 cloves garlic, chopped, or 2 tbsp. bottled, ready-to-use roasted or
 minced garlic.
Salt and Pepper to taste
3 tbsp. Port Wine
1/4 cup heavy cream
1/2 cup sour cream (light, nonfat, or regular)

Shake mushrooms in a bag with flour to coat lightly. Heat skillet over medium-high heat and add mushrooms, garlic, salt and pepper. Stir often for about five minutes. Add the port wine and cook one more minute. Turn off heat and stir in the cream and sour cream. Set aside.
*Enough sauce for 3 or four omelettes

Folded Omelettes

2 eggs for each omelette
Salt and pepper to taste

Beat eggs until the whites and yolks are blended. Heat a small omellete or sauté pan that is coated with oil or butter. Pour in eggs. As they cook over medium heat, lift the ends of the omelette with a pancake turner and tilt the skillet to allow the uncooked egg mixture to run to the bottom. When all is an even consistency, place a few spoonfuls of the mushroom sauce on the bottom half and fold the omellette in half, forming a half-moon shape.

Place on warmed plate and cover with more sauce. Repeat.

Tournedos Maconnaise

4 tournedos steaks, cut 1 to 1 and 1/2 inches thick
4 slices of bread, crust removed (for croutes)
6 tablespoons oil and butter mixed for frying

Sauce and Garnish
1 cup red wine
2 tablespoons butter
4 large flat mushrooms, stems trimmed level with caps
2 shallots, finely chopped
2 teaspoons flour
1/2 cup well-flavored beef stock
1 teaspoon tomato paste

Boil the wine until it is reduced by about one-third and reserve. Trim the bread for croutes the same size as the tournedos. In a heavy skillet heat half the oil and butter, fry the croutes until golden brown on both sides and drain on paper towels.

Wipe out the pan, heat the remaining oil and butter, and fry the tournedos briskly for 2 to 3 minutes on each side for rare meat, sprinkling with seasoning after turning them. Set them on a platter on top of the croutes and keep warm.

To make sauce and garnish, add 1 1/2 tablespoons butter to the pan and sauté the mushrooms gently on each side until tender. Place 1 on top of each steak. Add the remaining butter to the pan and cook the shallot gently until soft. Stir in the flour off the heat, pour in the reduced wine with the stock, bring to a boil, and simmer 2 to 3 minutes. Taste the sauce for seasoning. Spoon sauce and garnish over the tournedos and serve.

Veal Sweetbreads in the Basque Style

Not to be confused with "mountain oysters," sweetbreads are part of the thymus gland of a young calf. This delicacy pleased the epicureans of Campion's London as well as the earthy Basque herdsmen who created the wonderful recipe.

2 pounds veal sweetbreads
2 quarts water
1/4 cup distilled white vinegar
6 cups chicken broth
1 bay leaf
1 cup all-purpose flour, seasoned with salt and freshly ground pepper
6 tablespoons olive oil
3 cloves garlic, peeled and crushed
1 onion, diced
1 bell pepper, finely chopped
1 teaspoon paprika
Salt and coarse ground black pepper
1/2 cup reserved poaching liquid
1/2 cup freshly snipped flat-leafed parsley

Wash the sweetbreads and soak in the cold water and vinegar for 1 1/2 hours; drain. Poach the sweetbreads in the chicken broth and bay leaf for 15 minutes. Remove the sweetbreads and plunge into cold water. Save the poaching liquid for another use. Allow sweetbreads to cool; drain. Carefully pull off the clear membrane that coats the gland. Separate the sweetbreads into 1 1/2 inich pieces, discarding any gristle or fatty parts.

Dust the prepared sweetbreads in the seasoned flour. In a large frying pan, fry them in 3 tablespoons of the olive oil until lightly brown. Remove and set aside. Reheat the frying pan and add the remaining oil, the garlic, onion and bell pepper and sauté until just tender. Return the sweetbreads to the pan and add the paprika, salt and pepper and sauté all together. Add the reserved poaching liquid, cover, and cook gently for 5 minutes more, tossing about in the pan. Sprinkle with parsley just before serving.

A "WIMSICAL" PICNIC WITH LORD PETER

Quintessential Ham for the Monocled Epicure

Unnatural Death

Carve a ham as if you were shaving the face of a friend.

Henri Charpentier

I s it the kiss or the ham sandwich?

Let's start with the kiss. Now he may look a little ridiculous to us today. I mean what hunk wears a monocle? But in his own way Lord Peter is loaded with sex appeal. True, he was "a colorless shrimp of a child," and even his dear Uncle Paul, refers to him as "all nerves and nose," But Peter does possess a certain "body cleverness." He has beautiful hands for a horse; let us suppose that translates into some potential in the bedroom. And once "Flimsy" was discovered to be a great natural cricketer, "all his eccentricities were accepted as wit." Let's face it, in upper class England cricket rules.

So when the mysterious, turban-clad Mrs. Forrest blurts out, " No -- don't go yet -- I get so lonely, these long evenings," he assumes she wants him to make mad passionate love to her. Now, even though she is dripping in rings and makeup, she strikes Lord Peter as "essentially sexless." He is willing to make a stab at it, though, all for the sake of the case, the premature death of a very wealthy old woman.

Her bare shoulder is against him now and he takes the plunge.

> He pulled her suddenly and violently to him, and kissed her
> mouth with a practised exaggeration of passion. He knew then.
> No one who has ever encountered it can ever again mistake
> that awful shrinking, that uncontrollable revulsion of the flesh
> against a caress that is nauseous.

Lucky for him, he is the perfect gentleman and leaves before the potent veronal in his brandy leaves him at her mercy.

***

Now to the ham sandwich. . Sir Peter understands that eating is a fine art, and he uses that knowledge to ferret out the devious murderess in Dorothy Sayers' *Unnatural Death*. What appear to be the remains of a simple picnic shared by " a little waitress and her railway clerk," do not ring true to the monocled epicure. Something is wrong with the ham sandwich, for it is no ordinary ham that graces this repast.

> "The pig that was sacrificed to make this dainty tidbit fattened in no dull style, never knew
> the daily ration of pig-wash or the not unmixed rapture of the domestic garbage-pail.
> Observe," lectures Lord Peter, "the hard texture, the deep brownish tint of the lean; the
> rich fat, yellow as a Chinaman's cheek; the dark spot where the black treacle cure has
> soaked in, to make a dish fit to lure Zeus from Olympus."

For all his practiced passion and epicurean sensibilities, not to mention his great gobs of money and noble title, Sir Peter cannot do it alone. Certainly there is his good friend and now brother-in-law, Charles Parker, of Scotland Yard, "a quiet, sensible fellow" to play the foil. But it is Miss Climpson, one of those overlooked treasures of England, who is his ears and tongue. She is one of those "thousands of old maids, simply bursting with useful energy and magnificent gossip powers." With her cast iron stomach, she is able to withstand hour upon hour in tedious tearooms and ask questions a young man would never dare to.

So Lord Peter puts it all together, with the help of a thick-headed motorcycle rider who does not know the first thing about an air-lock in his feed.
Well, that can happen to the heart, too, can't it? An empty hypodermic injected into a main artery would stop the circulation without a trace.

***

With that quintessential ham sandwich as a centerpiece, let us pack a picnic worthy of our noble sleuth. But forget the woods with those grimy little ants and such. Bunter will pack up the picnic for us right here, in Sir Peter's London flat. Sit back in the huge chesterfield piled deep with cushions. Enjoy the brisk fire and take in the richness of the first editions in their old calf bindings "mellow and glowing in the lamplight."

Given Lord Peter's continental tastes and sophistication, I have taken the liberty to include some French side dishes to complete the menu. Top off your indoor picnic with *Golden Cheese Soufflé with Peppery Bacon,* and *French Potato Salad Bathed in Vermouth, Chervil, Chives and Tarragon.*

Before we can enjoy these sumptuous sides, let's get your meal off to a great start with some tips below on picking the *Quintessential Ham,* as well as an ode to the gastronomical delights of real *Dijon Mustard*

***

When buying a cured ham, choose one that is firm and plump. The meat should be finely grained and rosy pink. The exquisite Bradenham ham mentioned in *Unnatural Death* has been made since 1781 at Chippenham in Wiltshire, England. It is cured in molasses with juniper berries and spices to give it a sweet flavor and a perfectly black outside. A superb American choice is the Smithfield, one of the Virginia hams, which is dry-salted, smoked with hickory and apple wood, and then aged for at least a year.

Hailing originally from Dijon, France, this pale, grayish-yellow mustard is known for its clean, sharp flavor, which can range from hot to mild. Dijon mustard is made from brown or black mustard seeds, white wine, unfermented grape juice, and various seasonings.

The growing and preparation of mustard goes back to medieval courts where they often employed an official "mustardarius" to supervise this important gastronomical activity. In 1853 Maurice Grey invented a steam driver mustard mill in Dijon and founded the famous firm of Grey, now Grey Poupon.

"A true gastronome should always be ready to eat, just as a soldier should always be ready to fight."

Charles Monselet

Quintessential Ham Sandwiches

Use French croissants to cradle the ham, coating the flaky bread with plenty of rich butter, piquant Dijon mustard, and just a dash of horseradish. And insist upon the real thing--"coal-black, treacle-cured Bradenham ham."

Golden Cheese Soufflé with Peppery Bacon

6 slices bacon, diced
3 tbsp all-purpose flour
1/2 tsp salt
1/2 tsp dry mustard
1 cup milk
Few drops liquid red pepper seasoning
1 cup shredded Muenster cheese
6 eggs, separated
1/4 cup chopped parley

Sauté bacon until crisp in a small heavy saucepan; remove with a slotted spoon and drain on paper toweling. Pour off all drippings, then measure 3 tablespoons and return to pan. Blend in flour, salt, and mustard; cook, stirring constantly, just until bubbly. Stir in red-pepper seasoning; continue cooking and stirring until sauce thickens and boils 1 minute. Stir in cheese until melted; remove from heat. Let mixture cool while beating eggs. Beat egg whites just until they form soft peaks in a medium-sized bowl. Beat egg yokes until creamy-thick in a large bowl; blend in cooled cheese sauce, bacon, and parsley; fold in beaten egg whites until no streaks of white remain. Pour into an ungreased 8-cup soufflé or straight-side baking dish. Bake in moderate oven (350) 45 minutes, or until puffy-firm and golden-brown on top.

French Potato Salad Bathed in Vermouth, Chervil, Chives and Tarragon.

10 medium potatoes,
      boiled in their jackets
1 clove garlic
1 cup dry white wine
      or dry vermouth, heated
1/4 cup beef broth, heated
3 tablespoons tarragon or wine vinegar
1 1/2 teaspoons Dijon-style mustard
1/2 teaspoon salt
1/4 teaspoon pepper
1/2 cup olive oil
2 shallots, mined
3 tablespoons mixed chopped parsley, cervil, chives, and tarragon
Bibb lettuce or heart of romaine
1 to 2 tbsps capers (optional)

Peel potatoes and slice thin. Put in a bowl well rubbed with cut clove of garlic. Pour in wine and broth and let marinate for 1 hour. Pour off any excess liquid. Meanwhile, beat vinegar into mustard, salt, and pepper. Gradually add oil in slow stream, beating constantly. Add shallots and herbs to potatoes. Pour on dressing, toss gently with 2 wooden forks. Garnish with lettuce and capers.

Complete this elegant picnic with fresh strawberries dipped in whipped cream. Wash down with sparkling spring water, or a bottle of Veuve Clicquot Champagne.

NO FLIGHTS OF FANCY

Dinner with Defender of the Faith
Horace Rumpole

"Rumpole a la Carte"

Nouvelle Cuisine:

*It's so beautifully arranged on the plate –
you know someone's fingers have been all over it.*

Julia Child

Horace Rumpole does not think that eating is an art. He is thankful that *nouvelle cuisine* has not infected his home. Grateful, too, that his wife Hilda "cooks without any flights of fancy." Given a chop and a potato, she is "content to grill the one and boil the other. She can also boil a cabbage into submission and fry fish."

Which is fine for Rumpole, since he's not particularly thrilled with " wafer-thin slices of anything. " He's not rich enough to afford very small portions of food. Give him the good, plain cooking of She who Must Be Obeyed, as he affectionately calls Hilda, any day. That or the fried bread and bangers at the Taste-Ee-Bite café. Maybe a nice cigar with plenty of cheap red Chateau Thames Embankment served up at Pommeroy's Wine Bar. It keeps him regular and "blots out certain painful memories, such as a bad day in court in front of Judge Graves."

So his experience in "gracious living," as doled out as a night on the town with Hilda's rich Cousin Everard, is not Rumpole's cup of tea, so to speak. Frankly, the dinner at La Maison Jean-Pierre is a disaster.

> So we found ourselves in an elegantly appointed room with subdued lighting and even more subdued conversation, where the waiters padded around like priests and the customers behaved as though they were in church.

He stubbornly passes over *la poesie de la pointrine du canard,* and insists on "steak and kidney pudding, with mashed potatoes and a big scoop of boiled cabbage," Jean Pierre O'Higgins is not amused. He approaches Rumpole in the menacing manner of Irishmen who "stand far too close to you in pubs."

It seems that he is used to serving insults with his pricey portions. Warning our good lawyer not to commit any crimes in his restaurant, like ordering mashed spuds, Jean Pierre brags about the film stars he has sent away in tears "because they dared to mention Thousand Island dressing" in his presence.

The harangue is temporarily interrupted by the appearance of an "alarmed brown mouse" served up with other not as fresh delicacies at an adjacent table.

Thus it is a very subdued Jean Pierre who enters Rumpole's chambers a few days later. There's a little matter of Food and Hygiene Regulation 1970, which somehow finds the presence of live mice in an eating establishment rather worrisome.

Rumpole takes the case "in accordance with the great traditions of the Bar," but only after he tells the French Irishman that he has known many murderers who could teach him a lesson in courtesy. Crime is at least a more honest type of robbery than the prices at La Maison Jean Pierre.

Ferninand Isaac Gerald Newton, or Fig Newton, as he is known in the trade, is dispatched to watch over the staff of said establishment. And the Fig, "a lugubrious scarecrow of a man," comes up with the goods to clear the chagrinned chef.

Rumpole teases that "Knowing the law is a bit of a handicap for a barrister, " and clearly ignores Judge Graves at trial. Why does he always wind up with unsmiling fellows who "probably live on a diet of organic bran and carrot juice" and look at Rumpole as though he is "a saucepan that hadn't been washed up properly." Instead he goes after the hearts and minds of the jury. They should be concerned not with the law, but with justice. In spite of the dour Judge's admonition that Jean Pierre is technically if not literally guilty, Rumpole wins the case.

Hilda returns from her romp with tepid Everard through "all the restaurants with stars" in Bath and York. She has rather missed her "character" husband. Rumpole has missed her too. After all, "Life without a boss – that is --You were a great loss," he tells her.

All this joy calls for a celebration. And Rumpole knows just where he can get a dinner on the house. This time at La Maison Jean-Pierre he has no trouble placing his order for *Steak and Kidney Pud with Mashed Spuds on the Side.* Round out with more of Rumpole's favorites, like *Shepherd's Pie,* and close with that curiously named fruity pudding, *Spotted Dick.* Wash down with *Pommeroy's Chateau Thames Embankment.*

Part of the secret of success in life is to eat what you like and let the food fight it out inside.

Mark Twain

Steak and Kidney Pudding

Pastry

1 pound flour
1 heaping teaspoon baking
        powder
Pinch salt
9 ounces suet
1 1/8 cups water

Filling

1 1/2 pounds blade steak
        of beef
8 ounces of kidney
1 1/2 teaspoons fresh thyme leaves
1 tablespoon parsley stalks
Salt and pepper to season
Flour to dust
Water (approximately 10 fl. oz)

1. Measure flour, baking powder, salt, suet, and water for pastry.
2 Grease pudding bowl with butter.
3. Chop parsley stalks.
4. Cut meat and kidney into 1-inch cubes.
5. Measure thyme leaves, parsley stalks, and water.

Sift flour with salt and baking powder. Rub in suet or mix together in beater. Add the water and mix to a smooth dough. Take 2/3 of paste and roll out 1/2-inch thick. Line the pudding basin (7 inches diameter).

Combine the meat and kidney with seasonings, herbs, and a little flour. Pack the mixture into the basin until it comes level with the rim. Add sufficient water fill basin three quarter full.

Roll out the remaining paste, dampen the top of the crust in the basin, and lay on the top. Press the top on well and tie on a well-floured cloth, knotting the endings in the center.

Place in a large saucepan. Add cold water until it comes halfway up the basin. Fix a lid on top and boil gently for 3 hours. It is a good plan to put 2 marbles in the saucepan. When the water level gets very low they make a fearful din! When cooked, strip off cloth and serve from the basin.

Mashed Potatoes with Cabbage

6 medium potatoes
1/2 small had cabbage, shredded
6 scallions, chopped
1/4 cup water
1/8 teaspoons salt
1/3 to 1/2 cup milk
1/4 cup margarine or butter
1 teaspoon salt

Heat 1 inch salted water to boiling. Add potatoes. Heat to boiling; reduce neat. Cover and cook until tender, 30 to 35 minutes; drain. Heat cabbage, scallions, water and 1/8 teaspoon salt to boiling; reduce heat. Cover and simmer until crisp-tender, 5 to 10 minutes; drain.

Mash potatoes until no lumps remain. Beat in milk in small amounts. Add 1/4 cup margarine, 1 teaspoon salt and a dash of pepper; beat until potatoes are light and fluffy. Stir in cabbage and scallions; dot with margarine.

Shepherd's Pie

1 1/2 pounds lean, cooked roast lamb
3/4 ounce drippings or butter
2 medium onions, thinly sliced
1/4 cup all-purpose flour
1/2 teaspoon dry mustard
11/2 cups chicken broth
1/4 cup chopped fresh mint
1/4 cup chopped fresh parsley
1/2 teaspoon ground pepper
Salt, to taste
2 tablespoons Worcestershire sauce

Potato Topping

4 large potatoes, cooked and mashed
1/4 to 1/3 cup hot milk
1 ounce butter
Salt and pepper to taste

Brush an 8-cup capacity casserole with melted butter or oil. Preheat oven to moderately hot, 415 degrees. Trim meat and cut into small cubes, or grind.

Melt drippings or butter in a large pan. Add onions and cook until golden. Sprinkle in flour and mustard. Gradually add stock and blend, stirring until smooth. Bring gravy to boil, reduce heat, and simmer for 3 minutes.

Add the meat, mint, parsley, salt, pepper, and Worcestershire sauce and stir. Remove from heat and spoon into casserole.

To make topping, combine potato, milk, butter, salt and pepper. Mix until smooth and creamy. Spread evenly over meat; texture the surface with fork. Bake 40-45 minutes until heated through and potato topping is golden brown.

Spotted Dick (A Fruity Pudding)

1 1/3 cups all-purpose flour
1 1/2 teaspoons baking powder
1/2 cup sugar
1 1/2 teaspoons ground ginger
2 cups soft breadcrumbs
1/2 cup golden raisins
3/4 cup currants
1 1/2 cups ground or finely chopped suet
2 teaspoons finely grated lemon rind
2 eggs, lightly beaten
1cup milk

Serve with custard or cream. (See Morning Musings, p. 53)

Brush a 6-cup capacity pudding steamer or pudding basin with melted butter or oil. Line base with waxed paper; grease paper. Grease a large sheet of aluminum foil and a large sheet of waxed paper. Lay the paper over the foil, greased side up, and pleat it in the center. Sift flour, baking powder, sugar, and ginger into a large bowl. Add breadcrumbs, golden raisins, currants, suet and rind. Mix well with a wooden spoon.

Combine egg and milk; add to dry ingredients and mix well. Spoon mixture into prepared pudding steamer. Cover with greased foil and paper, greased side down. Place lid over foil, bring clips up and secure firmly with string or, if you have no lid, lay a pleated dish towel over the foil and tie it securely with string under the lip of the basin. Knot the four ends of the dish towel together, forming a handle to lower the basin into the pan.

Place the basin in a large, deep pan. Carefully pour boiling water down the side of the pan to come halfway up the side of the basin. Bring to a boil, cover and cook for 2 1/2 hours. Replenish with boiling water as the pudding cooks. Unmold pudding onto serving plate, cut into slices and serve with warm custard or cream.

***

Serve with Pommeroy's Ordinary Red, Chateau Thames Embankment, or Chateau Fleet Street, all favorite vintages of Rumpole. Of course, in reality, these are just fanciful names bestowed on the cheap red wine that is all that Rumpole's purse strings allow. Our California jug wines, as unpretentious as Rumpole, are a perfect substitute for those of us on the other side of the Atlantic. Follow with a savory cigar, and a volume of Wordsworth on the side.

CHIEF INSPECTOR MORSE'S FISH AND CHIPS TO DIE FOR

Wagner, Wordsworth and Worldly Wenches

The Wench is Dead

*Somebody forgot the corkscrew
and for several days we had to live on nothing
but food and water.*

W.C. Fields

Wine, women, and song, though not necessarily in that order.

And let's change out the wine for some good scotch, at least three fingers full for Chief Inspector Morse. Or maybe some nice frothy brew. Remember, it always tastes better when poor Sergeant Lewis pays the bill.

As for the women -- yes, he does have an eye for the ladies. And sometimes, only sometimes, a success. How unfortunate if he falls for the chief suspect and his last glance of her is when she is carted off by the authorities. But who knows. Potential murderess might even be a turn on. God help him, though, if her spelling is bad. We all have our hang-ups, you know. By nature, though, Colin Dexter's misanthropic detective is as self-described loner. He's just slightly more miserable than usual when surrounded by people.

As for song -- fleeting moments of contentment ride the waves of Wagner's *Die Walkure* blasting at full volume in his bachelor pad. Who needs companionship with a first edition of *A Shropshire Lad* (1896) tucked away securely on the shelves? Add a generous glass of scotch and life doesn't get any better. This comfortable routine is interrupted one Saturday morning when Morse is rushed to the hospital with a bleeding ulcer.

A young doctor interviews him in the Emergency Department of the John Raddcliffe Hospital complex. What about his drinking habits?

Morse is not quite candid, but who does tell these young interns God's truth, I ask you. "Two or three pints a day," and "scotch- sometimes I treat myself to a drop of Scotch." Further cross examination reveals that the bottled "drop of Scotch" lasts only a week to ten days, and is accompanied by a daily eight to ten cigarettes.

Wine, women, and song are about to be put on hold.

For his own good Morse is confined to a hospital bed above which is hung "a rectangular plaque bearing the sad little legend NIL BY MOUTH." Festivities are few and far between. He is cared for by a tight-lipped and sour-faced nurse:

> What's her name?
> They call her "Nessie."
> Was she born near the Lock?
> *In* it, Lewis.

Nessie is, indeed, a kind of Cerberus who screens the offerings his visitors bring him for any contraband food or drink. There are a few moments, however, with more compassionate hospital personnel, such as the "Fair Fiona." One particularly fine experience ends badly, however. Fiona comes to Morse's bedside and asks him to "unfasten his pyjama bottoms, to turn over on his lift side, and to expose his right buttock." Alas, all this is but a prelude to the intrusion of the terrible Nessie, who inserts a colorless liquid into his flank.

Then there is the "Ethereal Eileen" as Morse calls her. She looks "so good, so wholesome, in her white uniform with its dark-blue trimmings." And she handles his first encounter with a bedpan with such finesse. Such are the rather restricted romantic trysts of the invalid.

Lewis tries to liven up his day by smuggling in *The Blue Ticket*, a pornographic paperback which promises "Scorching Lust and Primitive Sensuality." But the misspellings somehow dampen his ardor. Instead Morse turns to some different reading material, *Murder on the Oxford Canal*, a case from 1859 involving the brutal murder and gang rape of one Joanna Franks.

Slowly he becomes obsessed with this long forgotten crime. From his bed Morse must prove that the two men hanged for the canal murder were innocent, exercising only, as Poirot called them, "the little grey cells."

The hospital fare, once he is able to eat again, consists of "one half-bowl of oxtail soup and a portion of vanilla ice-cream." Only in his clouded memory is Morse able to enjoy that decadent fried English classic, *Fish and Chips*, served up with plenty of grease and washed down with as many pints of ale as necessary. We've even thrown in a few other pub delicacies with those strange names, like *Toad in the Hole, Bubble and Squeak, and Bangers and Mash*. Eat up and enjoy. And don't forget to have Lewis pick up your tab.

Bubble and Squeak:

The substance and sustenance of this onomatopoetically dubbed dish are leftover vegetables which first boil (bubble) and the fry (squeak).

Mimi Sheraton

Fish and Chips

Vegetable oil
4 or 5 potatoes, cut lengthwise, into 1/2-inch strips
1 pound fish fillets, cut into 2 by 1 1/2-inch pieces
2/3 cup all-purpose flour
1/2 tsp salt
1/2 tsp baking soda
1 tbsp vinegar
2/3 cup water
Malt or cider vinegar
Salt

Heat oil (2 to 3 inches) in deep fat fryer to 375. Fill basket 1/4 full with potatoes; slowly lower into hot oil. (If oil bubbles excessively, raise and lower basket several times.) Use long-handled fork to keep potatoes separated. Fry potatoes until golden, 5 to 7 minutes. Drain potatoes; place in single layer on cookie sheet. Keep warm; repeat.

Pat fish dry with paper towels. Mix flour and 1/2 tsp salt. Mix baking soda and 1 tbsp vinegar. Stir vinegar mixture and water into flour mixture; beat until smooth. Dip fish into batter; allow excess batter to drip into bowl. Fry 4 or 5 pieces at a time until brown, turning once, about 3 minutes. Drain on paper towels.

Set oven control to broil at 550 degrees. Broil potatoes 6 inches from heat until crisp, 2 to 3 minutes. Sprinkle with vinegar and salt.

Toad in the Hole

1 cup all-purpose flour
1/2 cup self-rising flour
1/2 teaspoon salt
2 eggs, lightly beaten
1 cup milk
Salt
Coarse black pepper and Cayenne to taste
Pinch each ginger and nutmeg (optional)
8 thick, short sausages of your choice
1 3/4 ounces drippings
1 small onion, thinly sliced

Preheat oven to 400 degrees. To make batter, sift both flours and salt into a mixing bowl. Make a well in the center. Add combined eggs and milk gradually; whisk until smooth. Add seasonings. Set aside for 15 minutes.

Prick sausages all over with a fork. Place half the drippings in a shallow 6-cup capacity ovenproof dish. Place in oven to heat while preparing sausages. Heat remaining drippings in a large frying pan and cook the sausages for 5 minutes until well browned. Transfer to a plate; add onions to pan and cook for 3 minutes, until soft.

Arrange sausages and onion in the heated dish. Quickly pour batter over sausages and return to oven for 30 minutes, until batter is set and golden. Serve immediately with mustard.

Bubble and Squeak
(A pub owner's explanation for the dish's name lies in its effect on the digestive tract)

4 cups well-drained, cooked, chopped cabbage
1/3 cup butter
1 small onion, minced
2 cps diced boiled potatoes
Salt and freshly ground pepper

Put the cabbage in a colander and press out as much water as possible. Melt butter in a 10-inch skillet and brown onion. Add the cabbage and potatoes and toss until they start browning; season with salt and freshly ground pepper. Smooth mixture and cook until crusty and brown on the bottom. Invert on a heated platter and cut like a pie. Leftover diced or ground meat may be browned along with cabbage and potatoes.

Bangers and Mash

1 tablespoon oil
8 thick sausages
2 medium onions, sliced
2 tablespoons gravy powder
1 1/2 cups water
4 medium potatoes
2 tablespoons milk
1 ounce butter
Salt and pepper
Finely chopped parsley, for garnish

Prick the sausages with a fork. Heat oil in a large heavy-based frying pan; add sausages. Cook over medium heat for 10 minutes, until they are brown and cooked through. Transfer sausages to a plate covered with a paper towel.

Pour off most of the fat from pan, leaving about a tablespoon. Add oinions and cook over medium heat for 5 minutes until soft and golden. Combine gravy powder with water in a jug; stir until smooth. Add to pan; stir to combine with onions. Stir gravy constantly over a medium low heat for 2 minutes or until mixture boils and thickens. Return sausages to pan. Combine with gravy and serve immediately with mash.

To make mash, cook potatoes in a large pan on boiling water until tender; drain well. Mash with a potato masher until free from lumps. Add milk and butter; blend with a fork until smooth and creamy. Add salt and pepper to taste. Sprinkle chopped parsley over potatoes to serve.

CLASSIC CUISINE IN KINGSMARKHAM

Roast Beef and Yorkshire Pudding with Dora and Reg Wexford

Kissing the Gunner's Daughter

When mighty roast beef was the Englishman's food,
It ennobled our hearts and enriched our blood,
Our soldiers were brave and our courtiers good,
Oh! The roast beef of old England.

Richard Leveridg

Quite a grisly scene, their last supper. Three plates of food, cold and congealing, like the blood that sauces it. Yes, blood. Blood everywhere. A tide of red on the white tablecloth, the papered walls, the glowing lampshades, the rich carpet. It even sprinkles "the slices of French bread in speckles like currants."

Three are slaughtered. One survives.

> Something was crawling toward him out of the darkest part, where there was no lamp. It made a moaning sound. The phone lead was caught round it and the phone dragged behind, bouncing and sliding on polished oak. It bounced and jiggled like a toy on a string pulled by a child.

Well, not exactly a child. Daisy is all of eighteen, and suddenly an heiress. She's attractive, too. Even mild mannered Detective Chief Inspector Wexford is not immune to her charms. For a brief moment he fears he is in love with her and tries to imagine "her nakedness and wanting to make love to her."

And there are others, too. But not all of them are still alive. Step Grandpapa Harvey is fifteen years younger than his celebrity wife, and is "still a vigorous man." He can "start her off, initiate her," so to speak in the ways of lovemaking. An idea repulsive enough on its own, but doubly so when we learn it is grandmama's idea. Now grandfather, his progressive thinking wife, and enabling daughter are all dead.

Does Daisy's father, Gunner Jones, take umbrage with their proposed right of passage? We won't find out for sure until we have at least two more corpses, one hanged and one burnt, to add to our list.

No, Ruth Rendell's mysteries aren't cozy, bloodless academic exercises in logic. They do not end tidily with a sense of calm and order restored as the reader finishes the final page. Hers are stories that explore the disturbed psyches of murderers, revealing a world sometimes seedy, alarming, and repulsive. Her detective, then, must be a sea of calm.

Perhaps his very ordinariness sets Chief Inspector Reginald Wexford apart. He is not the pampered noble who solves crime for a hobby, the recluse who smokes tobacco stored in a Persian slipper, or the fluffy spinster living in a quaint village. Reg and Dora Wexford have been married for thirty years. They live comfortably in Kingsmarkham, having reared their two daughters, Sheila and Sylvia. He drinks Adam's beer, his wife dry sherry.

Wexford tries his best to be modern and liberal minded, especially when dealing with the chaotic love life of his adored Sheila, she with "such a lovely face, as perfect as Garbo's, as sweet as Monroe's." He endures her latest lover, "an odious young intellectual," with measured restraint, only calling him ugly and myopic to his wife. When the suitor glances at Dora's pearls and talks of the folly of older women believing such necklaces restore their lost youth, Wexford bites his tongue.

Television appearances for the chief inspector are no longer mysterious and frightening; he has gotten used to women driving and even owning automobiles. But he still thinks it unwise for a woman to go alone to answer a door in the evening. He rejects round ice cubes and superfluous mint leaves in cocktail drinks, and only reluctantly accepts "those unmarried couples who do everything together and put their names side by side on Christmas cards."

What else for a comfortable Sunday dinner but *Roast Beef with Yorkshire Pudding and Browned Roast Potatoes,* as thoroughly British and old fashioned as Wexford himself. Let's begin with *Hearty White Wine and Garlic Soup,* then on to *Fresh Mushroom Salad with Watercress and Scallions.* With our main course try a nice portion of *Leeks au Gratin,* and close with a dessert of exquisite lightness itself, *Melon with Strawberries and Anisette.*

Or if you prefer a heartier more traditional sweet, try *English Trifle with Fresh Raspberries and Sherry Drizzle, p. 41; Jammed Lemon Curd Tarts from a Derbyshire Market Town, p. 41; or Seed Cake Drenched in Cognac, p. 54.*

Only the pure of heart can make a good soup.

Ludwig Van Beethoven

Hearty White Wine and Garlic Soup

16 large garlic cloves, minced
4 tablespoons olive oil (or more)
1 cup dry white wine
6 cups bouillon
Salt to taste
1/4 teaspoon nutmeg
6 slices whole whet bread
3 egg yolks, beaten
3 egg whites, beaten stiff

Sauté the garlic in olive oil in a soup kettle for a few minutes. Add the wine, bouillon, salt and nutmeg, and bring to boil. Reduce the heat to low to medium, add the egg yolks, and cook for 15 minutes. Simmer for another 15 minutes, covered.

Place one slice of bread in each of six soup plates. Scatter the stiff egg whites over the bread. Ladle the hot soup over the bread and serve immediately

Fresh Mushroom Salad with Watercress and Scallions

1 tablespoon Dijon mustard (French, preferably)
1/4 cup olive oil
2 tablespoon apple cider vinegar
3 tablespoons chopped scallions
Salt and pepper to taste
1/2 pound fresh mushrooms
1 bunch watercress
1 head romaine lettuce

Place mustard and olive oil in a bowl and mis thoroughly with a wire whisk. Add the vinegar, scallions, salt, and pepper, and whisk again. Clean the mushrooms, slice thinly, and mix with the dressing. Chill until read to use.

Wash and drain well both the watercress and romaine lettuce. Break into bite-sized pieces. When ready to serve the salad, pour the dressing over and mix well.

Roast Beef

Place 5-pound beef roast fat side up on rack in shallow roasting pan. Sprinkle with salt and pepper. Insert meat thermometer so tip is in center of thickest part of beef and does not rest in fat. Do not add water.

Roast uncovered in 325 degree oven to desired degree of doneness: 125 to 130 for rare, about 1 3/4 hours; 140 to 150 for medium, about 2 1/4 hours. If desired, add potatoes after approximately 15 minutes. See directions for browned roast potatoes below. About 30 minutes before roast reaches desired temperature above, prepare Yorkshire Pudding Batter. Heat square pan, 9 x 9 x 2 inches, or oblong baking dish, 11 x 7 x 1 1/2 inches, in oven.

When roast reaches desired temperature, remove from oven; increase oven temperature to 425 degrees. Transfer roast to platter; cover lightly with aluminum foil. Pour off 1/4 cup drippings from roast pan; place drippings in heated square pan. Pour in pudding batter. Bake until puffed and golden brown, about 25 minutes. Cut into squares; serve with beef.

Yorkshire Pudding Batter

1 cup all-purpose flour
1 cup milk
2 eggs
1/2 teaspoon salt

Mix all ingredients with hand beater just until smooth.

Browned Roast Potatoes

8 medium potatoes
Salt

Wash and peel potatoes. Put them in a saucepan and barely cover with lightly salted water. Boil until half-cooked (about 10 minutes).

Drain potatoes and put them around roast that has already been in the oven for 15 minutes. Potatoes should cook for at least 45 minutes to 1 hour. Baste them with fat from meat. Turn potatoes occasionally during cooking and baste again to brown.

Leeks au Gratin

12 leeks
1 cup grated Gruyere (or similar) cheese
Butter
Salt and Pepper

White Sauce
4 tablespoons butter
4 tablespoons flour
2 cups milk
Dash nutmeg (optional)

Preheat oven to 350 degrees.

Select fresh leeks. Wash and clean them well, trimming them off at the top, where the leaves begin to get hard. Cook them in boiling salted water for 30 minutes. Rinse and drain them thoroughly.

Dissolve the flour in 1/2 cup milk. Melt the butter in a pan over medium heat. When it begins foaming, add the milk mixture, stirring continuously. Add the rest of the milk, and stir until the sauce comes to a boiling point. Lower the heat and continue stirring until the sauce thickens.

Butter an oblong baking dish and cover the entire bottom with 1 cup white sauce. Attractively arrange the leeks in the dish and cover them with the rest of the white sauce. Sprinkle the surface of the dish with the grated Gruyere cheese, salt and pepper. Bake at 350 degrees for 25 to 30 minutes.

Melon with Strawberries and Anisette

2 cantaloupe melons
1/2 cup sugar
4 tablespoons anisette
1 pint fresh strawberries, washed and hulled

Peel the melons and remove seeds. Cut in small slices and mash into a puree. Add the sugar and the anisette and mix everything thoroughly. Refrigerate for at least 2 hours.

Spoon the puree into chilled glass dishes and arrange whole strawberries on the top.

FRENCH COUNTRY FARE AND FOWL

Parisian Potluck with Edgar Allan Poe

The Murders in the Rue Morgue

*Poultry is for the cook
what canvas is for the painter.*

Brillat-Savari

C ould it be that the greatest of all English detectives, Sherlock Holmes, had American roots? Lurking there on Yankee soil -- the author at least --was the one who started it all. For it is Poe who created the prototype -- a mastermind detective working in competition with the police, a reclusive intellectual who examined clues in minute detail.

Romantic that he was, Poe was not content to house his sleuth this side of the Atlantic. For someone who gloried in the remote and exotic, what city had more of each than glorious Paris?

Like Holmes, Dupin shares rooms with another bachelor, but they are slightly, shall we say, irregular. The time-eaten and grotesque mansion which they rent is on the verge of collapse but perfectly suited for these "madmen of a harmless nature."

> At the first dawn of morning we closed all the massy shutters of out old building; lighted a couple of tapers which, strongly perfumed, threw out only the ghastliest and feeblest of rays. By the aid of these we then busied our souls in dreams -- reading, writing, or conversing, until warned by the clock of the advent of the true Darkness.

He and his narrator-companion make even the famously introverted Holmes seem a social butterfly by comparison.

> We lived completely alone. We had no visitors. I had kept the fact that I was living here a complete secret from my friends; and it had been many years since Dupin had given up going out in public. We existed within ourselves alone.

To Dupin "most men wore windows in their bosoms" and the things that went on inside of them are for him no secret at all. He easily eves drops on his companions' brainwaves, often surprising them with a terse reaction to their innermost thoughts. As with Holmes, all this is done through careful observation and deduction.

Like those great detectives of fiction who follow him, Dupin often outwits the police, finding them "too clever to be deep." Vidocq, the head of the Parisian police, is a good fellow and a hard worker, but he has little imagination. Like most of the Paris police, he is cunning but no more. He is a "good guesser." and may see one or two points with unusual clearness, but "there is such a thing as being too profound. Truth is not always in a well."

Dupin dismisses the police who " make a vast parade" of their proceedings. They have no method, or merely follow the method of the moment. Vidocq may have impressed many with his "master stroke of cant, *de nier ce qui est, et d'expliquer ce qui n'est pas*. (To deny what exists, and to explain what doesn't)," but it is Dupin who does just that.

Like Holmes with his cryptic intensity, and Poirot whose eyes turn a particular shade of green as he nears his quarry, Dupin speaks as though he were speaking to someone at a great distance when he is close on the scent.

> His eyes were vacant in expression; while his voice, usually a rich tenor, rose into a treble which could have sounded petulantly but for the deliberateness

and entire distinction of the enunciation.

In the musty darkness of their supposedly haunted mansion, Dupin unravels a case as graphically violent as any stealing today's "if it bleeds, it leads" headlines. A mother and daughter are brutally hacked to death. We find a razor besmeared in red, bloody clumps of human hair yanked out by the roots, and one of the corpses stuffed up the narrow chimney. Two forlorn bags of gold francs are the only eyewitnesses.

It is, however, the less sensational aspects of *The Murders in the Rue Morgue* that fascinate Dupin. He focuses on the superhuman strength of the killer, and the ghoulish voice of the murderer, who spoke French, Italian, Russian, or Spanish, depending on the witness. It all hangs on a broken nail, a small piece of ribbon, and a knot that is "peculiar to the Maltese."

Let us break into his seclusion and join Dupin in his cloistered dwelling, where simple yet elegant French country fare is the only interruption to his cogitations. We eat a simple French Boiled Dinner, *Pot au Feu* or "Pot in the Fire" recreated with all the authentic time honored flare.

Or perhaps, in celebration of his outwitting the baffled Paris police once again, we dine a bit more festively on *Chicken Edgar with Truffles Swimming in a Rich Wine Sauce* and *Fllufy French Cream Sauce over Fruit*.

Truffle:

"...this jewel sprung from a poverty-stricken soil"

Colette

Pot au Feu or "Pot in the Fire"

French Boiled Dinner

In this traditional recipe, the roast or poultry is stewed in its own broth with herbs, spices, and a healthy crop of vegetables. When done, the beef and vegetables are served separately from the broth, which is served steaming hot as a first course.

One pot and no risk of burning the dinner if the case makes Dupin lose track of time! A perfect supper for a detective of modest means.

1 1/2-pound beef boneless chuck roast
1 marrow bone (optional)
8 black peppercorns
1 teaspoon salt
1/4 teaspoon dried thyme leaves
1 bay leaf
4 cups water
1 1/2 pounds chicken drumsticks
10 to 12 small carrots
10 to 12 small onions or 3 large onions, cut in fourths
3 medium turnips, cut into fourths
4 stalks celery, cut into 1-inch pieces
3/4 tsp salt
1/8 tsp pepper

Place beef, marrow bone, peppercorns, 1 teaspoon salt, the thyme and bay leaf in Dutch oven. Add water. Heat to boiling; reduce heat. Cover and simmer 1 hour. Add chicken; cover and simmer 1 hour longer.

Add carrots, onions, turnips, and celery; sprinkle with 3/4 teaspoon salt and the pepper. Cover and simmer until beef and vegetables are tender, about 45 minutes. Remove chicken and vegetables to warm platter; slice beef. Strain broth; serve in soup bowls as a first course.

10 to 12 servings.

Chicken Edgar with Truffles Swimming in a Rich Wine Sauce

A main dish alternative in honor of Poe himself, this dish is as simple as it is elegant, features that favor both the inspector and his scribe.

3-ounces fresh black truffles, wiped clean, and thinly sliced
    or portobello or other mushrooms of your choice
2 tablespoons olive oil
1 teaspoon mined garlic
4 to 6 medium chicken breasts
1 can condensed cream of mushroom soup
1 cup dairy sour cream
1/2 cup Madeira or dry sherry
paprika

Place the chicken breasts, skin side up, in an 11x 7 x 11/2 inch baking dish.

Sauté the truffle or mushroom slices in the olive oil with the minced garlic until tender.

Combine with the other ingredients and pour over the chicken. Sprinkle generously with paprika.

Bake at 350 about 1 to 1 1/4 hours or till tender. Serve with hot fluffy rice,

Fluffy French Cream
Sauce over Fruit
(Creme Fraiche aux Fruits)

The noble *creme fraiche*--literally fresh cream--is a rich, heavy country cream with a tart flavor--similar to our dairy sour cream but richer and sweeter. The French use creme fraiche for many purposes--from thickening and enriching soups and sauces to garnishing desserts and pastries. This easy method of creating the cream enables you to produce a variety of fresh-fruit desserts in minutes.

2/3 cup whipping cream
1/3 cup dairy sour cream
2 to 3 cups assorted fresh fruit (blueberries, raspberries, strawberries or sliced peaches)
Ground nutmeg or sugar

Gradually stir whipping cream into dairy sour cream. Cover and refrigerate no longer than 48 hours. Sprinkle with nutmeg or sugar.

Serve fruit in large goblets topped with the *crème fraiche*, or layer in tall champagne glasses.

A ROYAL CHRISTMAS

In the Kitchen with Inspector and Ellery Queen

"The Adventure of the Dauphin's Doll"

We owe much to the fruitful meditation of our sages,
but a sane view of life is, after all, elaborated mainly in the
kitchen.

Joseph Conrad

He is truly an American sleuth. But don't confuse him with those hardboiled gumshoes popularized by Humphrey Bogart.

As his name suggests, he more closely resembles the aristocratic and cultured dilettante detectives of the cozy English mysteries. Ellery Queen is the title character and *nom de plume* of the writing team of Frederic Dannay and his cousin, the late Manfred B. Lee. Like plump cream puffs with their sweet custard oozing out, these mysteries are filled with scholarly allusions and enough Latin and French phrases to impress even medieval scholar Dorothy L Sayers, if not her noble sleuth, Lord Peter Wimsey.

Queen lives with his father, Inspector Queen, late of the New York Police department. The dynamics between the practical father and precocious son are not unlike those of TV's *Frazier*. Inspector Queen supplies professional connections and knowledge, leaving the masterful deductions to his brilliant progeny.

Not content to putter about the apartment in his well-earned retirement, we find Inspector Queen "in his kitchen, swathed in a barbecue apron, up to his elbows in *fines herbes*" making his gourmet turkey stuffing. This closely guarded recipe "calls for twenty-two hours of over-all preparation and some of its ingredients are not readily found at the corner grocer's." Our only other clues to its ingredients are the "bit of Turkey liver" deposited on the hand of estate lawyer Bondling when the inspector shakes his hand. We also overhear a cryptic reference to "Javanese black pepper and Country Gentleman Seasoning Salt."

Culinary pursuits must be ignored temporarily for the chance to catch their Nemesis, an American version of Holmes' Professor Moriarty, Comus, who, according to Ellery,

> Might be anybody. Began his criminal career about five years ago. He's... a saucy, highly intelligent rascal who's made stealing an art. He seems to take a special delight in stealing valuable things under virtually impossible conditions. Master of makeup – he's appeared in a dozen different disguises. And he's an uncanny mimic. Never been caught, photographed, or fingerprinted. Imaginative, daring--I'd say he's the most dangerous thief operating in the United States.

No wonder our wonder boy fails. We hardly have a propitious setting. What could be a scene of more unnerving unrest? Today we have road rage. What about shopper's psychosis? It is in a crowded department store on the last shopping day before Christmas, "traditionally the day of the inert, the procrastinating, the undecided, and the forgetful," where Ellery and Inspector Queen match wits with their villain.

Their carefully laid plans are foiled, and Comus succeeds in garnering his quarry, an ivory figure of a boy Prince wearing a forty-nine carat brilliant blue diamond in his gold crown.

***

But in the quiet dawn of Christmas morn Ellery too is enlightened. In typical armchair detective style, he solves the crime from the comfort of his living room, and with a few phone calls, easily apprehends the pompous perpetrator.

And what gastronomic delight to celebrate the triumph of his "little grey cells," as Poirot called them? It is a *Pastrami Sandwich*, resplendent with a dill pickle, which Ellery brandishes sword-like, as he retells his triumph. We have recreated his, New York Deli style, and added some traditional side dishes, such as *Kasha Varnishka* and *Cheese Knish*.

Our *Turkey Stuffing* is likely to please Inspector Queen, although his exact recipe is a closely guarded family secret. *Dinde des Artistes* is taken from the *Grand Dictionnaire de Cuisine*, 1873, by Alexandre Dumas. This recipe for turkey with a meat stuffing was dedicated to France's illustrious poets, whom Dumas thought had a special affinity for the culinary arts.

Turkey:

*One of the prettiest presents which
the Old World had received from the New.*

Brillat-Savarin

New York Deli Style
Pastrami Sandwich

The traditional pastrami sandwich is made with paper-thin slices of this highly seasoned smoked beef. Choose from among the many varieties of rye bread--from the dark German style to the lighter Jewish or Russian variety--to enclose the tender pungency the meat.

Complete with a dollop of horseradish and/or hot mustard. And don't forget the dill pickle on the side!

Kasha Varnishka

1 cup kasha buckwheat groats,
1 egg, well beaten
Cooking oil spray
2 tablespoons rendered chicken fat or vegetable oil
1 yellow onion, chopped
2 cups chicken broth
Salt and freshly ground pepper
1 cup pasta bow ties

In a small bowl, mix the kasha with the beaten egg. Be sure all the grains are covered with egg. Spray an iron skillet with cooking oil and turn to medium-high heat. Add the kasha to the pan and flatten it out, moving it around the pan until the egg dries and the grains have mostly separated. Set aside.

Place a pot of salted water on to boil for the pasta bow ties. (Do not cook them yet.)

In a 4-quart heavy stovetop covered casserole, heat the chicken fat or oil and sauté the onions until clear. Add the chicken broth and bring to a boil. Add the salt and pepper and the reserved kasha. Stir a bit and cover. Cook over low heat, stirring occasionally, until the kasha is tender, about 10 minutes.

In the meantime, boil the pasta just until tender. Drain well and stir into the kasha. Serve hot.

Cheese Knish

Cheese Filling

2 large yellow onions, chopped
4 tablespoons butter
12 ounces cream cheese, cut up
2 1/4 pounds dry-curd cottage cheese or farmer cheese

Sauté the onion in the butter until golden. Mix the onions in with the remaining ingredients, including any butter left in the pan, cover, and chill.

Dough

1 egg
1/4 cup salad oil
3/4 cup water
1 teaspoon distilled white vinegar
2 and 3/4 cups all-purpose flour

Place all the ingredients in the bowl of a heavy electric mixer. Mix with the dough hook until the dough is very smooth. Cover and allow the dough to rest for 15 minutes.

Divide the dough into 2 pieces. Roll out 1 piece of the dough into a very thin rectangle. Place a rope of the filling, about 3/4 inches in diameter, 1 inch away from the long edge of the dough. Fold the long edge of the dough over to enclose the filling; press to seal. Cut the filled roll away from the rest of the dough. Using the narrow edge of the handle of a table knife, press and cut the roll into individual Knishes, 2 inches long. Place the Knishes on oiled baking sheets. Repeat with the remaining dough and filling. Bake at 425 degrees, uncovered, until lightly browned, about 20 minutes.

Turkey with Meat Stuffing
Dinde des Artistes

Taken from the *Grand Dictionnaire de Cuisine*, 1873, by Alexandre Dumas, this recipe for turkey with a meat stuffing was dedicated to France's illustrious poets, whom Dumas thought had a special affinity for the culinary arts. "Dinde," meaning "of India" was an early name for turkey, reflecting the thinking that it came from the mysterious East.

1 15 pound turkey
Salt and pepper
2 cups fresh bread crumbs,
        soaked in milk
2 large onions, finely chopped
2 stalks celery, finely chopped
1 cup butter
1 pound veal, ground
2 cups ground chicken meat
1/2 pound sausage meat
1/2 pound blood sausage, casing removed
1 teaspoon dried sage
1/2 teaspoon dried thyme
1/2 teaspoon dried marjoram
2 tablespoons chopped parsley
2 eggs, slightly beaten
1 large can chestnuts in water, drained
1 cup chicken broth (optional)

Sprinkle turkey inside and out with salt and pepper. Squeeze out excess milk from bread. Simmer onions and celery in 3 tablespoons butter until transparent. Mix meat and herbs and work to a fine light mixture with the eggs. Crumble the chestnuts and add to stuffing. Stuff the turkey and truss. Spread with the one-half cup butter and sprinkle with salt and pepper. Cover with cheesecloth dipped in remaining butter, melted, and roast in a preheated 425 oven for 30 minutes. Lower heat to 350 and roast for 3 to 3 1/2 hours (about 20 minutes per pound), basting frequently. Test for doneness by moving turkey leg. If loose, bird is done. Remove cheesecloth; let turkey set for 15 to 20 minutes before carving. If desired, deglaze pan with chicken broth for pan gravy. Serves 14 to 16.

FOOD FOR THOUGHT
AT THE BLACK WIDOWER'S CLUB

White-Gloved Service with Henry

"No Smoking"
"Quicker than the Eye"
"Earthset and Evening Star"

*When you find a waiter who is a waiter
and not an actor, musician or poet, you've found a jewel.*

Andre Soltner

How do you do it, Henry? I don't mean the gourmet fare you serve. And it's not your uncanny and clever solutions. What I mean is how do you stand them? The members.

Isaac Asimov's *Black Widower's Club* short stories are obviously patterned after Agatha Christie's *Tuesday Club* series. A group of friends meets regularly for dinner, serving up tales of crime with their capons.

The supper party is replete with pompous writers, stuffy experts, and enough vanity and ego to fill Yankee Stadium. However, just as the meek and flustered Miss Marple consistently outwits all others in her shrewd apprehension of the small but significant detail, so Asimov's unobtrusive and thoroughly deferential waiter Henry regularly delivers the *coup de grace*.

Miss Marple's brilliant conclusions are tendered diffidently in between the stitches of her dancing knitting needles. Henry voices his deductions while serving cocktails, whisking away fine china, or pouring vintage brandy. With his "discreet smile" and an "unlined face which looks twenty years younger than his actual sixtyishness" Henry is "the club's redoubtable waiter." He accepts his brilliance at these monthly dinners with aplomb and characteristic humility:

> Of course, I lack a sense of the dramatic and, once the dramatic is discounted,
> it is possible to see the solution.

This austere brilliance is underscored by the large amounts of hot air generated by the pontificating pundits. They invariably focus on the esoteric points of the cases and miss the point entirely. Indeed, half the fun is to watch this odd assortment of male egos as they make complete fools of themselves.

The fact that Asimov based this series on the real-life Trap Door Spiders assemblage of friends and colleagues to which he belonged makes the reading even more humorous and bold, for no one but Henry is treated kindly.

"Dour-faced" Thomas Trumball, a cryptologist, "scowls with only his usual ferocity" as he welcomes the monthly guest with, "How do you justify your existence?"

Emmanuel Rubin, a prolific writer, intones behind thick-lensed glasses that he's "happened to have published over forty books."

Mario Gonzalo, the self-aware artist of the group sports "a crimson jacket, and subtly matching striped shirt," to say nothing of a "flowing scarf meticulously arranged to display the effect of casualness."

Attorney Geoffrey Avalon with his slanted dark eyebrows looks like "Satan in an amiable mood," and even Roger Halsted, "the soft-voiced math teacher," openly invites quarrels with fellow Black widowers. He makes them listen *ad nauseum* to his ongoing *magnum opus*--the entire *Iliad* in limerick form.

No doubt, Asimov has a little fun ridiculing himself as the "arrogant, vain, nasty, petty, and self-centered" guest mystery writer Mortimer Stellar in the cryptic publish or perish tale "When No Man Pursueth."

Egos aside, the conversation and the menu are always piquant at the Black Widower's club. Tonight let us enjoy the white-gloved service of the nonpareil Henry as he serves us *Iridescent Turtle Soup with Sherry on the Side* ("No Smoking"), *Veal Marengo in an Orange-Brandy Sauce,* ("Quicker than the Eye"), and *Black Forest Torte Besotted with Kirsch* ("Earthset and Evening Star").

I believe I once considerably scandalized her by declaring that clear soup was a more important factor in life than a clear conscience.

Saki

Iridescent Turtle Soup with Sherry on the Side

2 pounds turtle meat, cubed
3 bay leaves
2 sticks butter, unsalted
1/2 teaspoon oregano
1 cup all purpose flour
1/2 teaspoon thyme
1 cup celery, diced
1 teaspoon coarse black pepper
2 cups green onions, diced
1 1/2 cups tomato puree
1 quart chicken broth
1/3 cup fresh lemon juice
6 hard-boiled eggs, finely chopped
3 tablespoons minced parsley
Salt and pepper to taste
1 shot dry sherry per serving (optional)

In heavy saucepan melt butter. When melted add flour and cook until the flour turns the color of a penny. This roux must be stirred at all times so it will not burn. When roux reaches the desired color, add vegetables and turtle meat and cook until turtle is brown and vegetables are clear. Add the tomato puree and cook for about 15 minutes on low fire. In stockpot simmer beef stock. While boiling, add the mixture from saucepan and stir until soup is mixed and roux is dissolved. Stock should be smooth and have body. Simmer soup until turtle becomes tender, at which time you may add the lemon, diced eggs, and parsley. Each plate should be served with a shot of sherry on the side.

Veal Marengo in an Orange Brandy Sauce

1/4 cup corn oil
4 pounds well trimmed veal
       shoulder, cut into 1-inch
       cubes; or veal shank cut
       off the bone, trimmed well,
       and cut into 1-inch cubes.
Salt and pepper to taste
4 tablespoons butter
3 tablespoons flour
2 tablepsoons butter
3 onions, cut in half, and sliced
       into half moons
3 cups dry white wine
1 cup tomato puree
1 teaspoon tarragon
1/2 teasoon thyme
3 cloves garlic, minced
2 tablespoons brandy
1 3-inch piece orange rind
2 tablespoons butter
1 pound fresh mushrooms, quartered

Heat oil in a wide, heavy skillet. When hot, brown the veal on all sides. Do not crowd; do it in several batches if necessary. With a slotted spoon, transfer the browned veal to a deep heavy pot. Discard oil and any liquid from skillet. Season the veal with salt and pepper. Add the 4 tablespoons butter and let it melt over low hear. Sprinkle the flour over the meat and stir it over moderate heat for about 5 minutes.

Melt 2 tablespoons butter in the skillet; brown the onions. When the onions are browned, add the wine to the skillet. Boil rapidly for 2 to 3 minutes. Scrape up all the browned particles with a wooden spoon or spatula. Add the wine and onions to the veal. Add tomato puree, tarragon, thyme, garlic, brandy, and orange rind. Stir to combine everything well. If you are using veal shanks, wrap 2 of the bones in cheesecloth and add them to the pot.

Cover the pot and simmer over very low heat for 1 to 1 1/2 hours, or until the veal is very tender but not falling apart. Meanwhile, sauté the mushrooms in 2 tablespoons butter until they are tender and beginning to render their juices. Add the mushrooms and their juices to the tender veal. Remove shank bones. (The cooked marrow from the bones makes a delicious snack on toast).

Drain all the sauce from the veal into a saucepan. Cover the veal well to prevent drying out. Simmer the sauce rapidly until reduced to 2 cups and thickened. Combine the sauce with the veal and serve at once with white or wild rice.

Black Forest Torte Besotted with Kirsch

Cake

6 large eggs
1 cup sugar
1 teaspoon vanilla extract
4 ounces (4 squares) melted, unsweetened baking chocolate
1 cup flour, sifted

Beat eggs, sugar, and vanilla together until thick and fluffy, about 10 minutes. Alternately fold chocolate and flour into the egg mixture, ending with flour. Pour the batter into 3 8-inch cake pans that have been well greased and floured. Bake in a preheated 350-degree oven for 10 to 15 minutes or until a cake tester inserted in the center comes out clean. Cool cakes in pans for 5 minutes; turn out on racks to cool completely.

Syrup

1/4 cup sugar
1/3 cup water
2 tbsp kirsch liqueur

Make syrup by mixing together sugar and water and boiling for 5 minutes. When syrup has cooled, stir in kirsch. Prick the cake layers and pour syrup over all 3 layers.

Butter-Cream Filling

1 1/2 cups confectioners sugar   1
1/3 cup butter, unsalted
1 large egg yolk
2 tablespoons kirsch liqueur

To make the butter-cream filling, beat together sugar and butter until well-blended. Add egg yolk; beat until light and fluffy, about 3 to 5 minutes. Fold in kirsch.

Topping

2 cups canned sour cherries,
      drained
2 tablespoons confectioners' sugar
1 cup heavy whipped cream
1 8-ouncesemisweet chocolate bar

Cake Assembly

To assemble cake, place 1 layer on cake plate. Spread with butter cream filling. Using 3/4 cup of the cherries, which have been patted dry, drop cherries evenly over cream. Place second layer on cake. Repeat. Place third layer on top. Fold 2 tablespoons confectioners sugar into the whipped cream. Cover the sides and top of the cake with whipped cream. Decorate top of cake with remaining 1/2 cup cherries. To make chocolate curls from chocolate bar, shave (at room temperature) with a vegetable peeler. Refrigerate curls until ready to use. Press chocolate curls on sides of cake and sprinkle a few on the top. Chill until serving time.

MERRINGUE MYSTERIES

A Pub Crawl with Melrose Plant

The Lamorna Link

With beaded bubbles winking at the brim,
And purple-stained mouth;
That I might drink and leave the world unseen,
And with thee fade away into the forest dim.

John Keats

Some people think she's better than all three -- those grand dames of British mystery, Christie, Allingham, and Sayers. And a Yankee to boot! What is this world coming to?

Martha Grimes takes us on a literary pub-crawl. What with her books titled after pubs with names like the Dirty Duck, the Old Contemptibles, and the Horse You Came in On, who can resist? We sit around a blazing fire or amuse ourselves at the dartboard while Melrose Plant -- he only goes by Earl of Caverness when necessary -- plies the locals with free brew for information. He's not like his friend Richard Jury of Scotland Yard, with that natural charm that makes everyone tell him their life story . Especially the children. They are the hard ones for Plant. He has to use up endless supplies of sticky sweets to gain anything from the runny nose crowd.

Or not like Jury's assistant Wiggins. He uses cough mints and back soda biscuits to worm his way into witnesses' confidences. It's amazing how many hypochondriacs there are out there. And then there's Jury's sometime collaborator, Division Commander Brain Macalvie, with "eyes of a near-unholy cerulean blue, a hot blue that could strip you with a look." No one dares even breathe at a crime scene until he says so.

With these three competitors, no wonder Plant is looking for a little getaway. Actually, though, they are not the ones he is fleeing. And it's not Diana Demorney either, that vision in white with her long red nails wrapped around a Martini. Melrose doesn't mind her, even though she is scouting around for the next in her long line of husbands, and Melrose is terribly rich, you know. And he likes his other fellow carousers at the Jack and Hammer back home in Long Piddletown. Marshal Trueblood, an antique dealer as colorful as his wardrobe, conspires with Plant in endless schemes to stop the marriage of beautiful Vivian Rivington to an Italian Count they fondly call Dracula. The veritable girl next door, she is alternately linked with Jury or Plant in Grimes' series. While they go through quick changes of women with the dexterity of Vaudeville stars, she waits in the wings dallying with the count and an interminable engagement.

No, it is none of these characters that Melrose is fleeing. It is Dear Old Aunt Agatha. Just an aunt by marriage, and even less than that we find out. She is a shameless usurper from across the Atlantic who gobbles up Melrose's tea scones and helps herself to the family jewelry when she can.

Somehow Agatha has followed Melrose to the Cornwall countryside where his dreams of seclusion in a rented country estate quickly fade. She meets him at the Woodbine Tearoom where he enlists the help Johnny Wells, the local waiter/cab driver/amateur magician. He is to chauffer Aunt Agatha on a lark so Plant can view the property without her helpful comments.

> You won't want this, Melrose. Look at that thatch; you'll be needing
> a whole new roof. Whatever would you do with all of this rocky land?
> No, Melrose, it won't suit.

Melrose is soon to discover Johnny has still other talents. He is an incredible cook and makes his stay at the "Drowned Man, a typical country pub, but tipping its hat toward *inn,* since they let out rooms" much more bearable. Melrose can resist the highly touted fish fingers on the menu and have avocado baked with Roquefort, and cod with cucumber sauce that is "silky smooth and so fresh-tasting it might have leapt from the water and into the pan. "

Johnny confesses that he has learned his cooking skills from watching Chris, his beloved aunt. He lives with her and helps out with the baking of "meringues and scones and things" for the tearoom she runs with partner Brenda Friel.

When he gets home that night to help with the baking, the kitchen is still oven-warm. The long white porcelain table is covered with freshly baked cookies and scones. A sheet of meringues, lightweight and sweet, perhaps a bit too sweet for his taste, sits in the oven. But Aunt Chris is nowhere to be found.

Johnny enlists Melrose Plant to help him find this vanishing lady. Their search takes them to forlorn rocky outcroppings, a past tainted by pornography, snuff films, and innocent children drowning in the cold sea. But it is the meringues that hold the clue. Those left in his aunt's oven are not "a bit too sweet," as usual. It is a hand other than hers that has baked them. And Johnny knows just whose that is.

Let's try not to think about the twisted pornographers, the cold, drowned children, or the other corpses littering the Cornwell Coast. Instead, let's go down to the Woodbine Tearoom, where the "heather design on the polished cotton curtains, the faded roses on the chair cushions, the burned wood and the bay window's mullioned panes...blend like spices and mild honey into a satiny dough of contentment."

We can whip up some delightful *Meringues with Strawberries and Sabayon Custard*, just like Aunt Chris used to make. And they aren't a bit too sweet, either. But don't taste them before you whet your appetite with *Roquefort-Baked Avocados,* and dine on *Cod* "that might have leapt from the water into the pan" *Smothered in Cucumber Sauce.* And hold off on the *Old Peculiar* and take Johnny's recommendation for wine, too. A fine crisp white *Bordeaux.*

A good meringue puts up a light crunchy resistance before it effects a melting disappearance between tongue and palate... to alight in the brain as a poem.

Anonymous pastry chef

Roquefort-Baked Avocados

4 large ripe avocados
Juice from one lime
8 ounces well-aged Roquefort Cheese
8 to 10 slices thick-cut bacon
4 tablespoons dry red wine
1 small can sliced black olives
1/4 cup sun flower nuts (optional)
Coarse-ground black pepper

Cut the avocados in half and remove pits. Squeeze lime juice onto avocados to keep from turning brown. Arrange on foil-lined baking dish.

Cook the bacon in the red wine until almost crisp. Drain on a paper towel, pat dry, and crumble into pieces. Set aside.

In a small mixing bowl, gently toss the Roquefort cheese and olives.
Scoop the cheese mixture into the concave portion of each avocado. Sprinkle with the crumbled bacon and top with sunflower nuts.

Bake in a moderate oven (350 degrees) until avocados are warm and cheese is melted, about 15 minutes. Or microwave at 50% power for 3 minutes.

Cod Smothered in Cucumber Sauce

Warm Cucumber Sauce

3 large cucumbers, peeled and halved lengthwise
Salt
1 1/2 tablespoons butter
1/4 cup diced green onion
1/2 cup sour cream
1/4 cup dry white wine
2 tablespoons snipped fresh dill

Scoop out seeds from the cucumbers and cut crosswise into slices about 3/8 inch thick. Sprinkle with salt and let drain in a colander for at least 15 minutes. Rinse and press out excess liquid.

Melt the butter in a large skillet and cook the green onion until soft and transparent. Add the cucumbers and cook until tender yet firm, about 5 minutes. Stir in the sour cream, wine, and fresh dill.

Cold Cucumber Sauce

2 cups peeled, finely chopped and drained cucumbers
1 cup mayonnaise
1 cup sour cream
1/2 teaspoon grated green onion
1/2 teaspoon crumbled dill weed
1 tablespoon lemon juice
Salt and pepper, to taste

Combine all ingredients and mix well. Chill before serving.

Baked Cod Fillets

2 pounds cod fillets, rinsed and patted dry
Coarse ground black pepper to taste
Spray on cooking oil

Spray cooking oil onto a shallow baking dish and arrange 2 pounds of cod fillets in it. Dot with butter. Sprinkle with the black pepper. Cook in a slow oven, about 325 degrees for 20 minutes. * Pour the cucumber sauce over the partially cooked cod and continue baking another 15 to 20 minutes, until fish flakes with a fork.

*Or bake the cod the full 35 to 40 minutes and top with the cold cucumber sauce.

Meringues with Strawberries and Sabayon Custard
Meringues

6 egg whites
1 teaspoon vanilla
1/4 teaspoon cream of tartar
Dash salt
1 cup sugar

Have egg whites at room temperature. Add vanilla, cream of tartar, and salt. Beat till frothy. Gradually add sugar, a small amount at a time, beating till very stiff peaks form and sugar is dissolved.

Cover cookie sheet with plain parchment paper. Drop shapely dollops of meringue onto the prepared baking sheet with a soup spoon. Bake in very slow oven (275 degrees) for 1 hour. Turn off heat and let dry in oven with the door closed about 1 hour.

Sabayon Custard

Aunt Chris's recipe for this light and delectable custard has its roots not in France, as one might suspect from its name, but in Renaissance Italy. In 1533 Catherine de' Medici became the bride of Henry II of France and brought as part of her dowry a team of exquisite Florentine cooks. Zabaglione, a hot, foamy custard, was steeped in the sweet, fortified Marsala wine of Sicily. Sabayon is the French translation of this delicious dowry. We will follow Aunt Chris's variation and use Madeira wine, but not quite "so much, you could get drunk off it," as Johnny remembers.

6 egg yolks
3 tablespoons sugar
6 tablespoons Madeira
     (You can substitute Marsala or sweet sherry, if you like)

Place egg yolks in the top of a double boiler and beat with a rotary or electric beater. Gradually add the sugar and beat until foamy. Place over 1 inch of simmering water. Add wine (traditionally, half an eggshellful of wine per yolk). Beat until mixture triples and is very thick and hot.

To serve cold, pour hot custard into a bowl. Set in a larger bowl of ice and beat vigorously until cold and thick. Chill until ready to serve.

Assembly

1 pint strawberries, washed and hulled.
     (If they are especially large, you may want to halve or quarter them)

Now just follow Johnny's instructions. Pile strawberries on a meringue and pour the hot or spoon the chilled custard over them.

COOKING WITH CORPSE POWDER

Navajo "Sole" Food

The Dark Wind

Appetite, a universal wolf.

William Shakespeare

The body is in pretty bad shape. The soles of the feet are cut away. And the hands too. What's left of the body, "mostly a tattered ragbag of bare bone, sinew, gristle, and a little hard muscle," is rotten. It's enough to make you lose your appetite.

And if you're Sgt. Jim Chee of the Navajo Tribal Police you're already squeamish about corpses. I mean, a Navajo isn't even supposed to mention the name of a dead person unless he wants to risk waking the living dead. No wonder Sgt Chee's breakfast is a little on the dry side. The crusty *piki* bread tastes of wheat and bacon fat in his mouth. It is thin and hard. The coffee from his stainless-steel thermos is at least hot. But them you don't want a lot of fancy grub when you're ruminating on mutated corpses.

Or maybe he picnics on the contents of the canvas pack he keeps next to his bedroll behind the seat of his pickup. A can of corned beef and crackers can keep him going for quite a while in an emergency. The pretty young waitress who brings him "Hopi Stew" at the Hopi Cultural Center draws some comment. The stew does not. For the more formal occasions there is good company and more elaborate tableware.

> The boy came in and put a white coffee mug on the floor beside the old man. He handed Cowboy a Styrofoam cup and Chee a Ronald McDonald soft drink glass. The light of the kerosene lamp gave his waxy white skin a yellow cast and reflected off the thick lenses of his wire-rimmed glasses.

So much for the fine china and tinkling teacups. Even the coffee is horrible. It is instant, "boiled in water which tasted a little of gypsum and a little of rust from the barrel in which it was stored."

But when you're looking for a possible witch in the barren Hopi mesas of Arizona, eating is your last concern. You might indulge in a little conversation, Navajo style:

> Chee said nothing. West was an old hand at communicating with Navajos. He would talk at his own pace until he said what he had to say, without expecting the social feedback of a white conversation.

You trust you instincts and what your uncle told you about tracking. You remember how to estimate the age of a doe by reading the splaying of its cloven toes. Or how to test the moisture in a drying mud ridge of dirt to see how old the tire tracks are.

And you drink in the stark beauty of the land. Out here, the nearest movie show is a hundred miles away and most people don't have electricity. Back Mesa is virtually roadless, almost waterless. "A dozen major dry washes and a thousand nameless arroyos drain away runoff from its bitter winters, and the brief but torrential 'male rains' of the summer thunderstorm season." The sun is hot, even in early morning, and the smell of dust is in your nostrils. Dust. There is always dust.

And you keep your ears open for talk about witch craft and corpse powder. The witches make it out of the skin that has the individual's soul stamped on it, "like on your palms, and fingers, and the soles of your feet, and the glans of your penis." You know about the Ya Ya Society that initiates people into sorcery, those who want to become "two-hearts"

Are you a little scared when you drive up to his house, the one that belongs to this maybe member of the Ya Ya Society? The sun is down now, only a "streak of fire." The place looks deserted, the house mostly in ruins, and the small kiva used by men for ceremonial meetings, broken and rotted. This sacred place seems as "dead as the men who built it so long ago."

But here, from the waxen lips of the twelve-year old albino boy standing in its doorway, from Taylor Sawkatewa, old and toothless, you begin to learn the truth. The truth that will link the disturbing clues that blow around the mutated corpse like the dark wind of the desert. Chee, you can now begin to understand an "airplane's mysterious crash in the nighttime desert, a bizarre attack on a windmill, and a vanishing shipment of cocaine."

It all ends in a pounding rain. Revenge, retribution, and renewal wash through the desert gorges. They take away the taste of dry, dusty death. At least for now.

Perhaps Sgt. Chee's appetite returns with this flood. Does he long for something more than corned beef in a can with crackers? Might he wash it down with something other than instant coffee tasting of rust? We have conspired to cook up something extra tasty for our favorite tribal policeman. Wrap your dry lips around moist and meaty *Navajo Kneel Down Bread, Hopi Venison Stew, Navajo Blue Hominy Posole, and Peach Crisp with Pinon Nuts.* Sgt. Chee might be persuaded to trade his black coffee for a sweet, syrupy coke or if, and only if, the case is closed, a frosty can of cold beer. Tecate with a twist of lime.

*Better a dry morsel and quietness therewith, than
a house full of sacrifices with strife.*

Proverbs 17:1

Navajo Kneel Down Bread

So named because the cook had to kneel down to tend this pit-baked bread. Our version saves the kneecaps and uses the oven. Here we have a more creative use for Chee's ubiquitous canned corned beef hash.

5 ears fresh corn
1 12-ounce can corned beef
1/2 cup chopped fresh green chilies, peeled and seeded, or 1 4-ounce can
1 egg, lightly beaten
Corn husks, soaked in water

Scrape corn from cob into a mixing bowl. Add corned beef, chilies, and egg. Mix well. Pat husks dry and lay out, with overlapping edges, to form a 7 x 12-inch rectangle. Place corn mixture in the middle of the rectangle and form into a loaf. Fold husks over loaf and tie with string or wrap in aluminum foil. Place on a baking sheet and bake in a preheated 350 degree oven for 60 to 75 minutes, until loaf is cooked and set. Unwrap, slice and serve.

Hopi Venison Stew

Chee seems more interested in the pretty waitress who brings him this dish at the Hopi Cultural Center than the stew itself. We hope our version, with the piquant green chilies, captures his attention.

2 pounds venison, cut into 1 1/2-inch cubes
1/2 cup unbleached flour
1/4 cup vegetable oil
1 medium onion, chopped
1 cup diced celery
1/4 cup hot or mild fresh green chilies or a combination of the two,
  peeled, seeded, and diced. (Or half a 4-ounce can)
4 cups water
1 tablespoon dried Mexican oregano
1 1/2 cups sliced carrots
2 potatoes, peeled and cut into 1/2-inch cubes
1 cup diced yellow turnip (rutabaga)

Pat venison dry with a clean towel and dredge lightly in flour. Heat oil in a large skillet and brown the meat well on all sides. Transfer meat to a stew pot or Dutch oven. In the same oil, sauté onion, celery, and chilies until onion is translucent. Add vegetables to the pot along with water and oregano.

Bring stew to a boil. Reduce heat to low, cover, and simmer for 1 1/2 to 2 hours, until meat is almost tender. Add carrots, potatoes, and turnips. Cook an additional 20 to 30 minutes, until potatoes are tender.

Navajo Blue Hominy Posole

Maybe Chee would be happier with this hearty stew from his own tribe. The term " posole" refers to the major ingredient in this recipe, whole blue hominy, as well as the dish itself.

2 cups blue posole (dried whole hominy)
1/2 cup mild fresh green chilies, roasted, peeled and chopped, or
      1 4-ounce can
1 to 3 fresh or canned jalapenos, peeled, seeded, and chopped (May be
      decreased to 1 jalapeno, or eliminated entirely for a milder flavor.)
1/2 cup chopped onion
2 cloves garlic, minced
1 peeled, seeded, and chopped tomato
2 to 3-pound boneless pork roast
2 teaspoons dried Mexican oregano (optional)
Salt, to taste

Rinse posole in cold water until water runs clear. Soak it for several hours in cold water. Place posole with water to cover in a large pot or Dutch oven. Bring to a boil over medium-high heat. Reduce heat to low and simmer, covered, until posole pops, about 1 hour.

Add chilies, jalapenos, onion, garlic, tomato, and pork. Simmer, covered, about 4 hours until meat is tender. Shred meat and return it to the pot. Season with oregano and salt. Simmer, covered for at least 1 additional hour.

Peach Crisp with Pinon Nuts

According to legend, it was a starving Hopi woman who taught the Navajos how to cultivate peaches. They planted them in the sheltered areas of Canyon de Cheely's high cliffs, which reflected the heat of the sun and kept the winds away.

6 large ripe peaches, peeled, pitted, and sliced
1/4 cup granulated sugar
1/2 teaspoon cinnamon
3/4 cup unbleached flour
3/4 cup light brown sugar
1/4 teaspoon salt
1/2 cup butter
2 tablespoons pinon nuts

Preheat oven to 375 degress. In a 1 1/2 to 2 quart baking dish, toss the peaches with granulated sugar and cinnamon. In a mixing bowl, combine flour, brown, sugar, and salt. Cut in butter until the mixture resembles coarse meal. Sprinkle this mixture evenly over the peaches. Sprinkle the top with nuts. Make for 30 to 40 minutes, until golden brown on top.

Sgt. Chee likes his with generous scoops of Cool Whip or vanilla ice cream.

Index

Tarte Bourbonnaise, 44
Tarte Suisse with Pine Nuts and Fresh Swiss Chard, 47
Vegetable Pulao, 28
Watercress Fennel Salad with Tarragon-Rosemary Vinaigrette, 21
Wild Rice and Pecan Pilaf, 13

Soups
Creamy Oyster Soup, 78
Hearty White Wine and Garlic Soup, 126
Iridescent Turtle Soup with Sherry on the Side, 150

Sup at the Pub
Bangers and Mash, 119
Bubble and Squeak, 119
Fish and Chips, 118
Shepherd's Pie, 111
Steak and Kidney Pud with Mashed Spuds, 110
Toad in the Hole, 118

Suppers Supreme
Brandied Pate de Foie Gras Pie, 11
Chicken Edgar with Truffles Swimming a Rich Wine Sauce, 135
Cod Smothered in Cucumber Sauce, 160
Golden Rissoles with a Port Cumberland Sauce, 136
Hopi Venison Stew, 168
Kasmiri Griddle Kabobs, 28
Oven Roasted Christmas Turkey with Chestnut Stuffing. 79
Pan Seared Venison with Wild Mushrooms and Chili Glaze, 12
Pot au Feu (Pot in the Fire), 134
Roast Christmas Goose with Apricot-Port Glaze, 20
Roast Wild Duck with Orange Gravy, 62
Roast Beef with Yorkshire Pudding, 127
Smothered Pheasant in Sherry Cream Sauce, 11
Sole Marguery in Wine Sauce, 86
Tournedos Macconnaise, 95
Turkey with Meat Stuffing (Dinde des Artistes) 144
Veal Marengo in an Orange Brandy Sauce, 151
Veal Sweetbreads in the Basque Style. 96

Sweets
Apple Cream Steeped in a Lemon, Thyme, and Rosemary Wine Sauce, 88
Birnennwecken Pear Cake, 45
Blanc Mange in Custard Sauce, 38
Black Forest Torte Besotted with Kirsch, 152
Crème Fraiche aux Fruits (Fluffy French Cream Sauce over Fruit), 135
Drunken Strawberries Featuring a Fruity Young Pinot Noir, 46
English Trifle with Fresh Raspberries and Sherry Drizzle, 54
Grand English Plum Pudding, 80
Grape Raita with Cilantro, Mint, and Green Chile Spiked with Yogurt, 30

CPSIA information can be obtained
at www.ICGtesting.com
Printed in the USA
LVOW03s1149031215

465189LV00003B/44/P

9 781589 394995